# 兴利除害 富国惠民

## ——新中国水利60年

Generate Benefits and Mitigate Hazards to Contribute
to the Prosperity of the Nation and the Interests of the People
—— 60 Years' Water Development in China

中华人民共和国水利部 编

Compiled by the Ministry of Water Resources, P. R. China

# 献给

# 中华人民共和

For the 60th Anniversary of the Fou

国成立60周年

ding of the People's Republic of China

为庆祝中华人民共和国成立60周年，水利部组织编撰了这本《兴利除害　富国惠民——新中国水利60年》画册，既是对新中国60年治水成就的回顾和展示，也是对未来水利发展的憧憬和展望。

我国幅员辽阔，地形多样，气候复杂，水资源时空分布不均匀，水旱灾害频发。在中华文明的历史长河中，治水兴水历来是兴国安邦的大事。新中国成立以来，党和政府带领人民开展了波澜壮阔的水利建设，取得了举世瞩目的伟大成就。我们以占全球约6%的径流量、9%的耕地，保障了占全球21%人口的温饱和经济发展，并向全面建设小康社会迈进，水利发挥了极其重要的作用。

60年来，我们战胜了1954年长江大水、1963年海河大水、1991年江淮大水、1994年珠江大水、1998年长江松花江嫩江大水、2003年和2007年淮河大水以及2006年川渝大旱等历次特大洪水和严重干旱灾害，成功应对了频繁发生的台风和山洪灾害袭击，夺取了2008年抗御低温雨雪冰冻灾害和水利抗震救灾斗争的重大胜利。

60年来，全国江河堤防从新中国成立之初的4.2万千米增加到28.69万千米，以长江三峡、黄河小浪底、淮河临淮岗为代表的重点水利工程相继建成并发挥效益，我国大江大河主要河段基本具备防御新中国成立以来最大洪水的能力，中小河流具备防御一般洪水的能力，重点海堤设防标准提高到50年一遇。

60年来，各类水库数量从1200多座增加到2008年的8.6万多座，总库容从约200亿立方米增加到6924亿立方米，开展了大规模病险水库除险加固，南水北调等一大批水资源优化配置工程陆续开工建设，全国水利工程年供水能力达到7491亿立方米，累计解决了2.72亿农村人口的饮水困难和1.65亿农村人口的饮水不安全问题。

60年来，全国农田有效灌溉面积从2.4亿亩扩大到8.77亿亩,占全国耕地面积48%的灌溉面积上生产了占全国总量75%的粮食和90%以上的经济作物。节水灌溉面积已经达到全国农田有效灌溉面积的41.8%,在连续30年保持农业灌溉用水量零增长的情况下,扩大有效灌溉面积1.2亿亩,粮食产量提高近50%。

60年来,累计治理水土流失面积101.6万平方千米,建成农村水电站近4.5万座,解决了3亿多无电人口的用电问题,通过小水电代燃料工程有效保护了生态环境。水生态修复逐步拓展,黄河连续10年不断流,塔里木河、黑河、石羊河生态逐年恢复。

60年来,初步形成了比较完善的涉水法律法规体系和规划体系,依法治水管水深入推进,水利改革取得重大突破,水利科技创新日新月异,水利信息化和现代化水平不断提高,节水型社会建设取得显著成效。

水资源是基础性的自然资源和战略性的经济资源,是生态与环境的控制性要素。以水资源的可持续利用保障经济社会的可持续发展,是当今世界各国的共同使命。我国人多水少、水资源时空分布不均、与生产力布局不相匹配的基本水情将长期存在,特别是在全球气候变化影响日益明显和工业化、城镇化进程不断加快的新形势下,我国水资源领域的问题更加凸现,治水任务依然艰巨。

站在新的历史起点上,我们要顺应经济社会发展的新要求、水资源条件的新变化、水利实践的新发展、人民群众的新期盼,以科学发展观为指导,认真贯彻中央水利工作方针,积极践行可持续发展治水思路,坚持以人为本,坚持人与自然和谐,坚持可持续利用,坚持统筹兼顾,坚持改革创新,坚持现代化方向,大力发展民生水利,进一步加快水利基础设施建设步伐,持续提升水利对经济社会发展的保障和支撑能力;坚定不移地实行最严格的水资源管理制度,明确水资源开发利用红线、水功能区限制纳污红线、用水效率控制红线,加快推进供水管理向需水管理转变,全面建设节水防污型社会;加大重点领域和关键环节改革攻坚力度,积极推进水资源管理体制、水利投融资体制、水利工程建设运行机制、水价形成机制等方面的改革,加快构建充满活力、富有效率、更加开放、有利于科学发展的水利体制机制,加快推进传统水利向现代水利、可持续发展水利转变,实现水利事业更长时间、更高水平、更好质量的全面发展,以水资源的可持续利用保障经济社会可持续发展。

是为序。

中华人民共和国水利部部长

2009年9月

# Preface

To celebrate the 60th Anniversary of the Founding of the People's Republic of China, the Ministry of Water Resources has compiled the book "Generate Benefits and Mitigate Hazards to Contribute to the Prosperity of the Nation and the Interests of the People — 60 Years' Water Development in China" in which the achievements in water sector in the past 60 years are reviewed and presented, and the water development in the future is looked ahead.

With a vast territory, diverse topography and a complex climate, China is faced with uneven distribution of water in time and space and frequent flood and drought disasters. In the long history of Chinese civilization, water management has always been the priority of the government. Since 1949, the Chinese government has made great efforts on water management and achieved remarkable results which enabled China to feed 21% of the world population with 6% of world water resources and 9% of arable land, and stride on its way to a moderately prosperous society.

For 60 years, we have successfully fought against catastrophic disasters including the Yangtze River flood in 1954, Haihe River flood in 1963, Haihe River flood in 1991, Pearl River flood in 1994, and Yangtze River, Songhua River and Nenjiang River flood in 1998, Huaihe River floods in 2003 and 2007 and serious drought in Sichuan Province and Chongqing City in 2006, frequent typhoons and flash floods as well as the freezing ice rain disaster and secondary disaster following Wenchuan Earthquake in 2008.

For 60 years, the total length of dikes has increased from 42,000 km in 1949 to 286,900 km at present. Key projects, including the Three Gorges Project, Xiaolangdi Water Project and Linhuaigang Water Project have generated great benefits. Main sections along major rivers and lakes are able to withstand the biggest flood ever occurred after 1949 and small and medium-sized rivers can defend ordinary flood while key coastal levees can hold flood with an occurrence of 50 years.

For 60 years, the number of reservoirs has increased from 1,200 to 86,000 in 2008 and the total storage capacity has risen from 20 billion $m^3$ to 692.4 billion $m^3$. A large number of risky reservoirs have been reinforced and water allocation projects including the South-to-North Water Transfer Project have been constructed. Annual water supply capacity has gone up to 749.1 billion $m^3$. The Chinese government has provided drinking water to 272 million rural population and clean drinking water to 165 million rural population.

For 60 years, effective irrigated area has increased from 240 million *mu* to 877 million *mu* accounting for 48% of the national farmland and producing 75% of grain and 90% of cash crops. Irrigated area with water-saving facilities has accounted for 41.8% of total effective irrigated area. With a zero increase of water usage in agricultural irrigation for consecutive 30 years, effective irrigated area has been expanded by 120 million *mu* and grain output increased by 50%.

For 60 years, 1.016 million km$^2$ of water-and-soil loss area has been brought under control and 45,000 hydropower stations have been built in rural China providing electricity to 300 million population. Through "the Replacing Firewood with Small Hydropower Project", the environment has been successfully protected. The Yellow River has realized non-running dry for consecutive 10 years. Ecology of Tarim River, Heihe River and Shiyang River has gradually been rehabilitated.

For 60 years, water law and legislation system of relative perfection has been formed. Water management according to law has been promoted. Marked breakthrough has been achieved in water management reform. Great innovation has been achieved in water science and technology. Water management has incorporated more information technologies. Remarkable progress has been made in the establishment of water-saving society.

Water is a basic natural resource and strategic economic resource. It is a controlling factor for ecology and environment. To ensure sustainable socio-economic development with sustainable water management is a mission that shall be shouldered by countries around the world. The situation that China has large population but little water unevenly distributed in time and space and does not match productivity layout will exit in the long run. With stronger impact of climate change and accelerated industrialization and urbanization, water problems become more acute and water challenges more critical.

Looking forward from a new horizon, we should meet the demand of comprehensively building a moderately prosperous society, stick to principles of putting people's interests first, harmony between human and nature, sustainable utilization, overall planning, reform, innovation and modernization, further accelerate the construction of water infrastructure and "10 important projects" which highlight people's interest and reinforce the supporting role water has played in socio-economic development. We should steadfastly implement the most strict water management system, specify the base lines for water development and utilization, pollutant carrying capacity of water functioning zones and water utilization efficiency, speed up the transform of supply-oriented water management to demand-oriented water management and the build-up of a water-saving and pollution-prevention society. We should strengthen reform in key areas, promote reform in water management system, financing system, project construction and operation system and water pricing system and build a highly efficient, more open and scientific water management scheme full of vitality so as to realize a long-term, comprehensive and sound development of water cause and ensure sustainable socio-economic development with sustainable water utilization.

Chen Lei, Minister of Water Resources, P. R. China

September 2009

序

| 第一篇 | 自然与历史 | 1 |

基本水情
治水历史

| 第二篇 | 建设与成就 | 51 |

大江大河治理
城乡供水保障
农田水利建设
水土流失治理
生态文明建设
水能资源开发

| 第三篇 | 防灾与减灾 | 143 |

洪涝灾害防控
干旱灾害防御
极端天气应对
水利抗震救灾

| 第四篇 | 管理与改革 | 173 |

水利规划
水利法治
水资源管理
节水型社会建设
工程建设与管理
水文信息服务
队伍建设

| 第五篇 | 科技与创新 | 209 |

科技创新能力
重大科技成果
技术引进推广
国际合作交流
水利信息化

后记

# Contents

Preface

Chapter I  Natural Conditions and History ... 1
      The Characteristics of Water Resources
      History of Water Management

Chapter II  Construction and Achievements ... 51
      Harnessing and Training of Major Rivers and Lakes
      Provision of Water Supply for Urban and Rural Areas
      Farmland Infrastructure Construction
      Water and Soil Loss Control
      Construction of Ecological Civilization
      Development of Hydro Resources

Chapter III  Disaster Prevention and Mitigation ... 143
      Prevention and Control of Floods and Water-logging
      Prevention and Resist of Droughts
      Counter Measures for Extreme Weather Conditions
      Prevention of Earthquake Caused Water Disasters

Chapter IV  Management and Reform ... 173
      Programming and Planning of Water Projects
      Legislation in Water Management
      Water Resources Management
      Building of Water-saving Society
      Projects Construction and Management
      Provision of Hydrological Information
      Capacity Building

Chapter V  Science, Technology and Innovation ... 209
      Capacity of Science and Technology Innovation
      Important and Significant Achievements
      Promotion and Extension of New Technologies
      International Exchanges
      Information Technology

Epilogue

# 第一篇 自然与历史

我国位于欧亚大陆东部，地势西高东低，呈阶梯状分布。地形多种多样，由山地、丘陵和高原组成的山区面积约占国土总面积的2/3，平原和盆地等约占1/3。由于幅员辽阔、经纬跨度大、距海远近不一、地势高低不同、地势地貌及山脉走向各异，因而气温降水的组合复杂多变，形成了多种多样的气候。从气候类型上看，东南部属季风气候，西北部属温带大陆性气候，青藏高原属高寒气候；从温度带划分看，有热带、亚热带、暖温带、中温带、寒温带和青藏高原区；从干湿地区划分看，有湿润地区、半湿润地区、半干旱地区和干旱地区。我国特殊的地理气候条件导致水旱灾害非常严重，洪涝、干旱、台风、山洪、泥石流等灾害多发，2/3的国土面积可能发生各种类型、不同程度的洪水，大部分地区面临不同程度的干旱威胁。在中华文明的历史长河中，治水历来是安民兴邦的大事。

# Chapter I
# Natural Conditions and History

China is located in the eastern part of Euro-Asian continent, characterized by a ladder-like physical feature with high west and low east. China enjoys a diverse topography. Mountain areas, hills and rugged plateaus occupy 2/3 of its total territory whereas plains and basins take the rest. Due to different geographical location and topographical features, wide scope in both latitude and longitude, mountain ridges, etc. China has various climate featuring different weather, temperature and precipitation. In terms of climate, east China has monsoon climate, northwest temperate continental climate, Qinghai-Tibetan Plateau high frigid climate. For temperature belt, China has tropical, subtropical, warm-temperate, mid-temperate and cold-temperate belts. Besides, the vast territory of China can also be divided into humid, semi-humid, semi-arid and arid areas. The distinct topographical conditions also result in serious flooding and drought disasters. China experiences frequent flooding, drought, typhoon, flash flood and mudflow. 2/3 of China is prone to flooding of different type and magnitude, while most China is threatened by drought. In the long history of Chinese civilizations, disaster prevention has always been one of the top agenda.

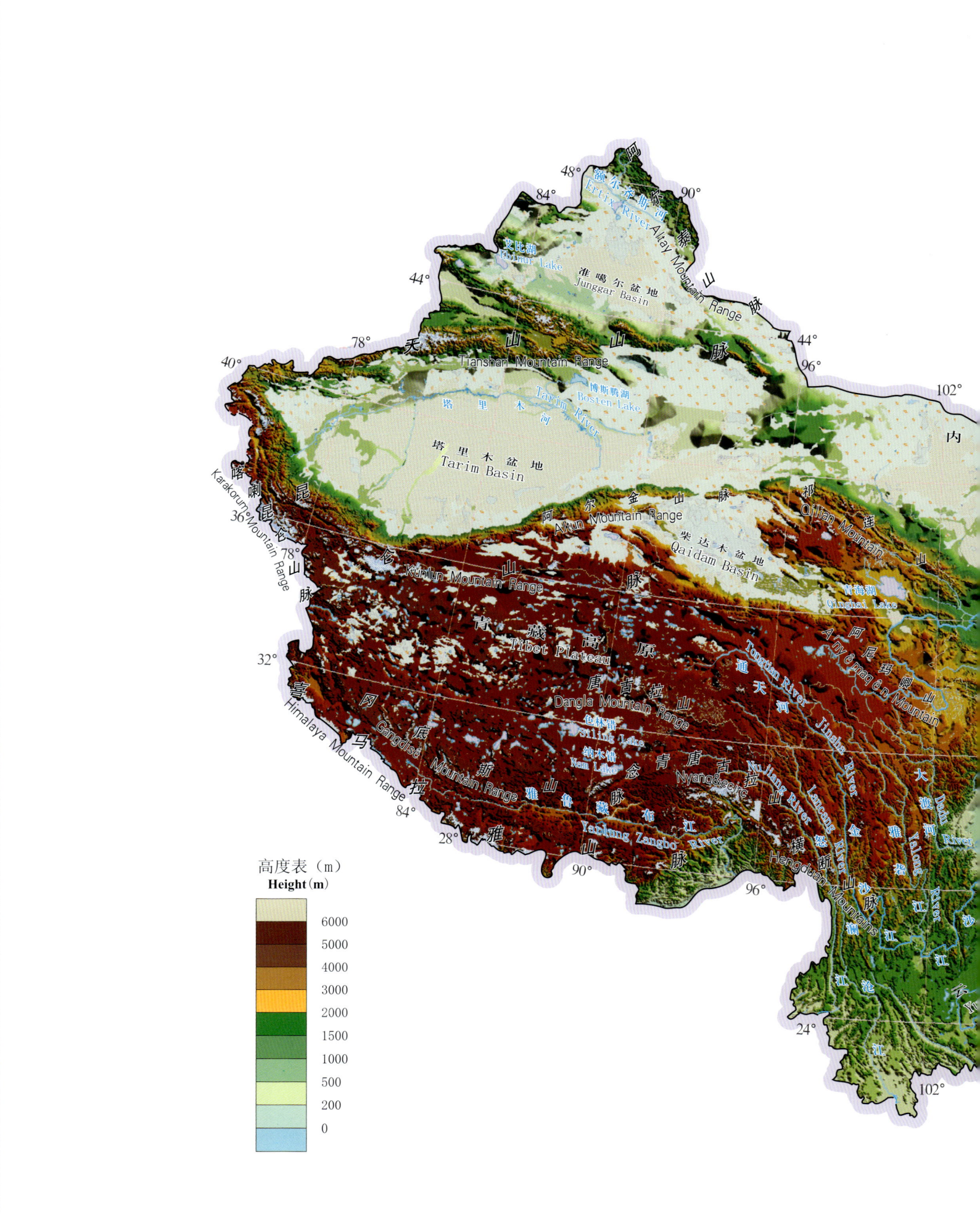

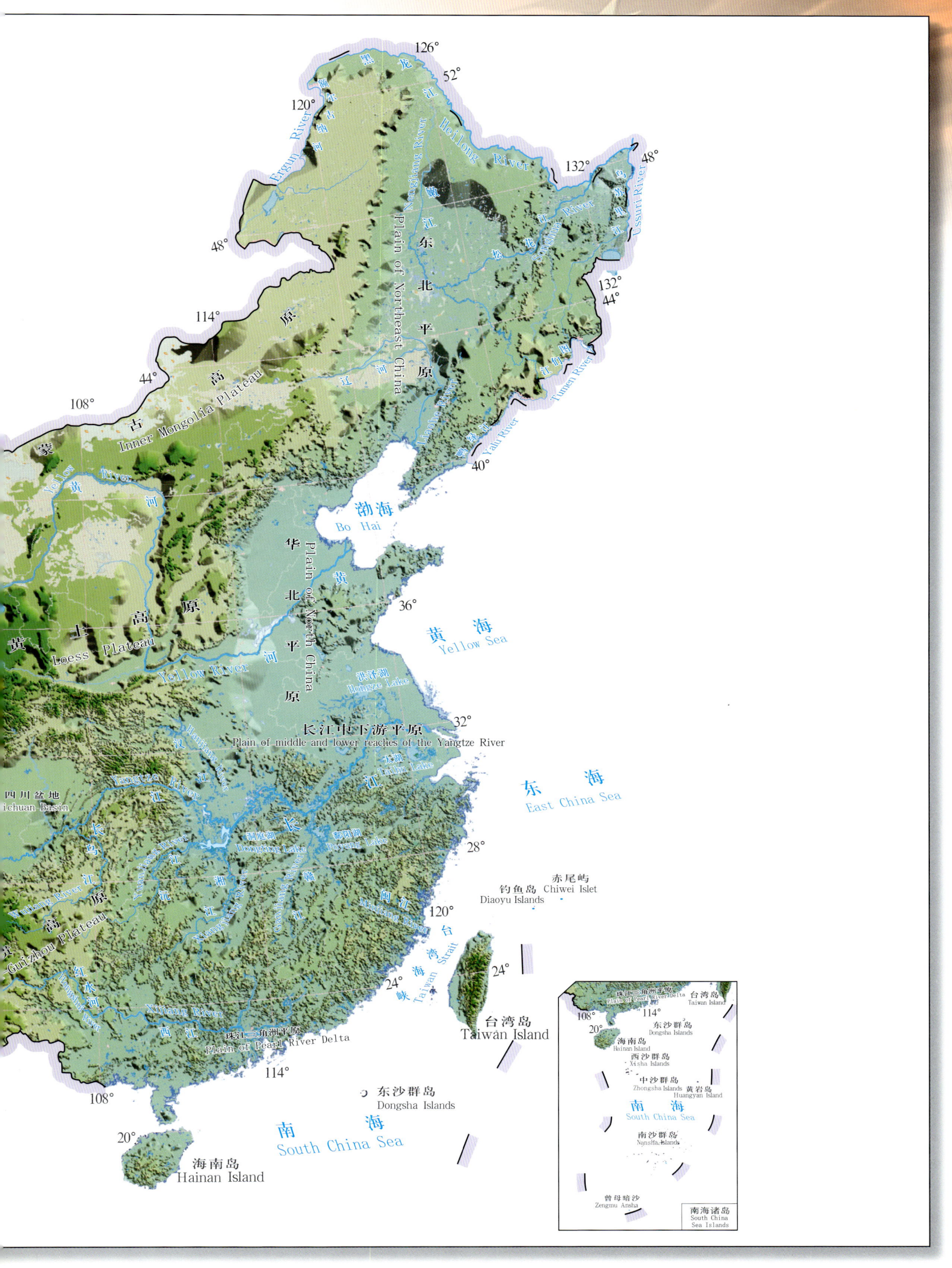

我国地势地貌图
Topographical Map of China

## ◆ 基本水情
### The Characteristics of Water Resources

我国降水和水资源的时空分布很不均匀，与人口、耕地和经济社会发展的格局很不相称。年降水量空间分布的规律是：从东南沿海向西北内陆递减，沿海多于内陆，南方多于北方，山区多于平原。降水量的季节分配特征是：南方雨季开始早，结束晚，雨季长，集中在5～10月；北方雨季开始晚，结束早，雨季短，集中在6～9月。冬季，大陆受西伯利亚干冷气团的控制，气候寒冷，降水稀少。夏季，受海洋气流的影响，降水丰富，暴雨频发。降水量的年际变化因地区而异，多雨区年际变化较小，少雨区年际变化较大；沿海地区年际变化较小，内陆地区年际变化较大，而以内陆盆地年际变化最大。丰水年的降水量是枯水年的2～8倍。全国陆地多年平均年降水总量为61775亿立方米，折合平均年降水深为650毫米，小于全球的平均值800毫米。我国多年平均年径流总量为27388亿立方米，多年平均地下水总量为8128亿立方米，水资源总量约为2.8万亿立方米，人均水资源占有量约为2100立方米，约占世界人均水平的1/4，是全球人均水资源最贫乏的国家之一。

Precipitation and water resources are unevenly distributed in time and space in China, which differs from the layout of population, arable land and social-economic development. The rainfall amount is decreased from the southeast coast to the northwest inland, and the rainfall in mountain areas is more than that in plains. The rainy season in the south starts earlier, with a longer period from May to October, comparing that from June to September in the north. In winter, influenced by cold air mass from Serbia, weather is cold and precipitation is less. Summer usually witnesses frequent strong rainfall due to marine current. Distinct changes in annual rainfall could be perceived in areas with little rainfall, inland area, particularly inland basin area. The precipitation in wet years is 2-8 times more than that in dry years. The total average annual precipitation in China is 6,177.5 billion m³, and it can be converted into the average annual precipitation depth of 650 mm, which is less than world average of 800 mm. The total average annual runoff in China is 2,738.8 billion m³, and the total average amount of groundwater is 812.8 billion m³. The total quantity of water resources is 2,800 billion m³. Average amount of water resources per capita is 2,100 m³, which is only 1/4 of the world average. China is one of those countries with least average amount of water resources per capita.

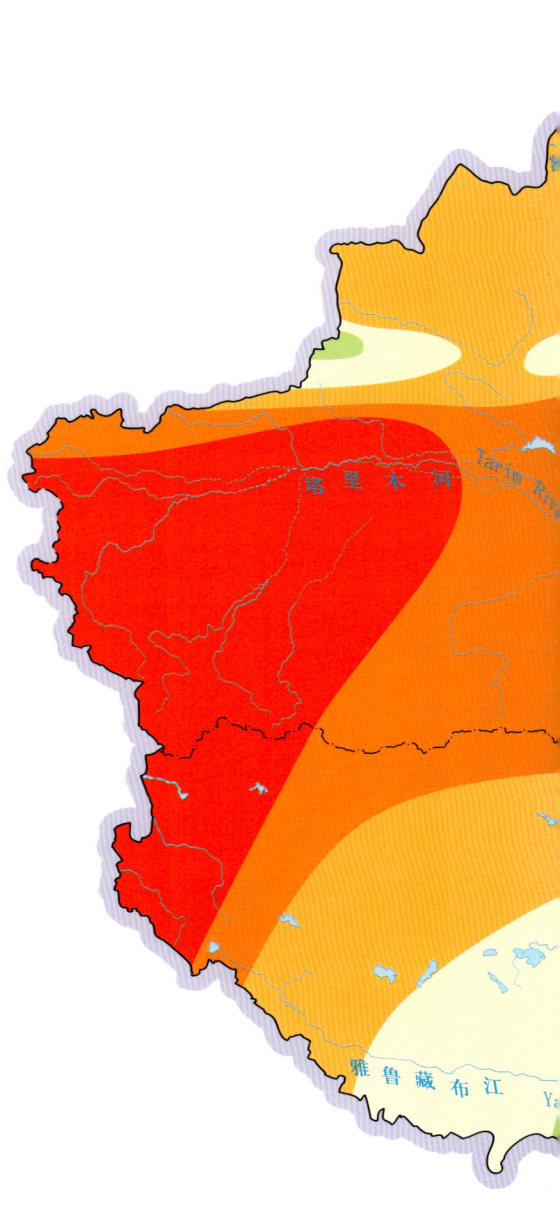

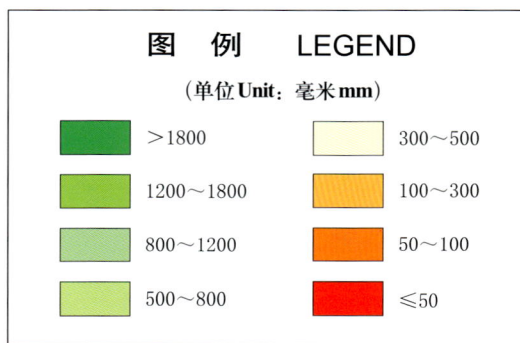

台湾省资料暂缺
Temporary lack of Taiwan Province information

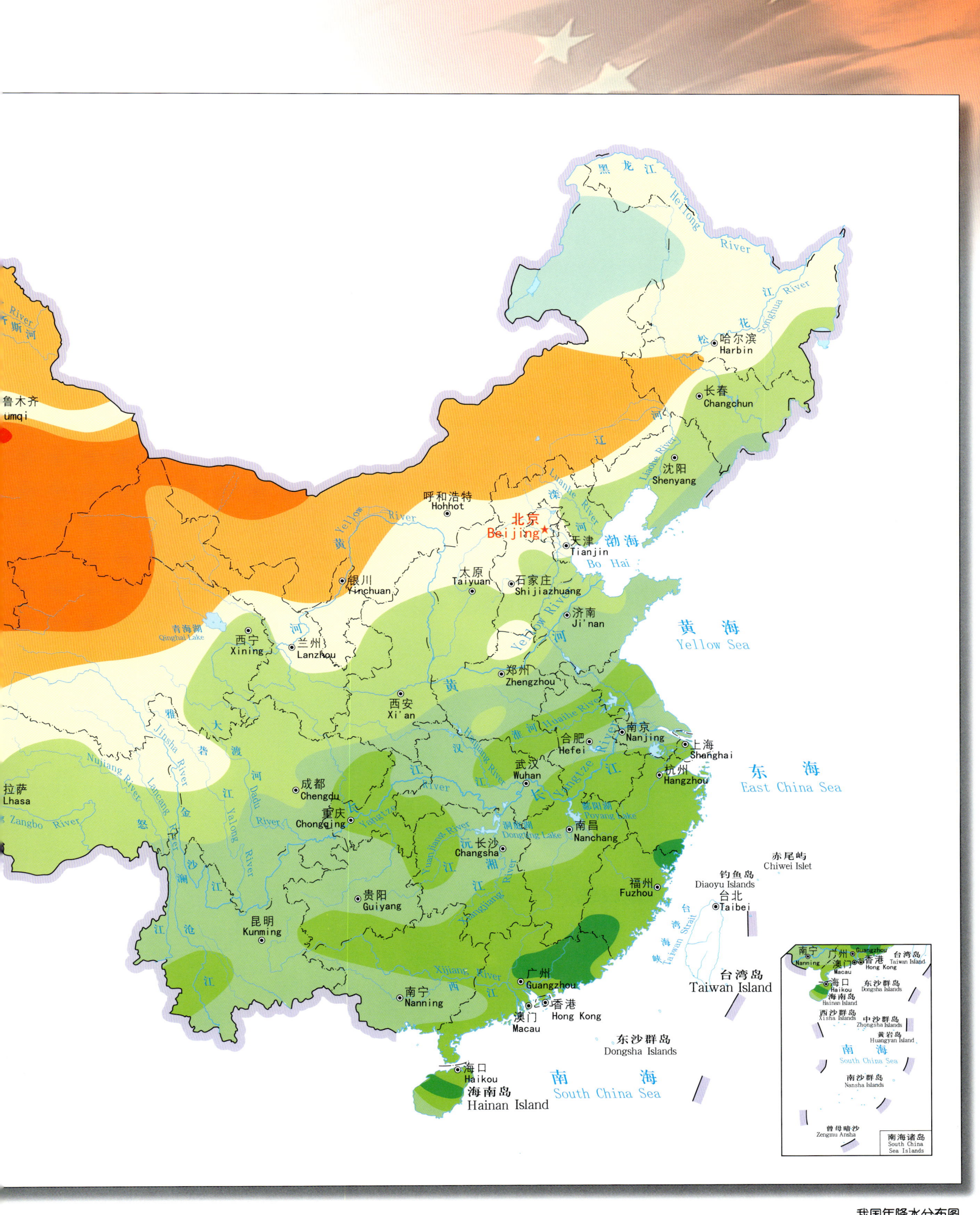

我国年降水分布图
Map of Annual Rainfall Distribution

我国江河纵横交错。河流总长度约为42万千米，流域面积超过100平方千米的河流有5万多条，超过1000平方千米的河流有1500多条。受地形和气候条件的影响，以大兴安岭、阴山、贺兰山、祁连山、巴颜喀拉山、唐古拉山、冈底斯山一线为界，分为东南部的外流区和西北部的内流区。外流河大多呈东西走向，以太平洋为归宿，夏季多处于汛期，冬季进入枯水期。东南沿海有众多独流入海的中小河流。内流河多为季节性河流，其主要补给类型为冰雪融水和山地降水，夏季水量较丰富，冬季水量减少甚至断流。西北内陆地区河流稀少，有面积广大的无流区。我国有众多跨国界河流，包括边界河流和流出流入国境的河流。在众多河流中，长江、黄河、淮河、海河、珠江、松花江和辽河被称为"七大江河"。其中长江、黄河是中华文明的主要发祥地。

Running crisscrossed, China has a great number of rivers with a total length of 420,000 km. Over 50,000 rivers has a catchment area above 100 km$^2$, more than 1,500 rivers' catchment area exceed 1,000 km$^2$. Influenced by topography and climate conditions, a line drawn from Daxing'anling to Helan Moutain, Qilian Mountain, Bayankala Mountain, and Tanggula Mountain and all the way to Mount Kallash has separated China into southeast outflow area and northeast inflow area. Most outflow rivers run from the west to the east and empty themselves into the Pacific Ocean. Summer is usually flood season, while winter is dry season. In southeast coastal area, there are a number of medium and small rivers which flow into the sea. Most inflow rivers are seasonal ones, whose sources are snow melt and rainfall from the mountainous areas. For these rivers, runoff is abundant in summer, but decrease or even run dry in winter. Northwest inland China has very few rivers. China has several international rivers, including boundary rivers and rivers run through the country border. Among all the rivers in China, Yangtze River, Yellow River, Huaihe River, Haihe River, Pearl River, Songhua River and Liaohe River are together called "the 7 Largest Rivers". Yellow River and Yangtze River are the major cradles of Chinese civilization.

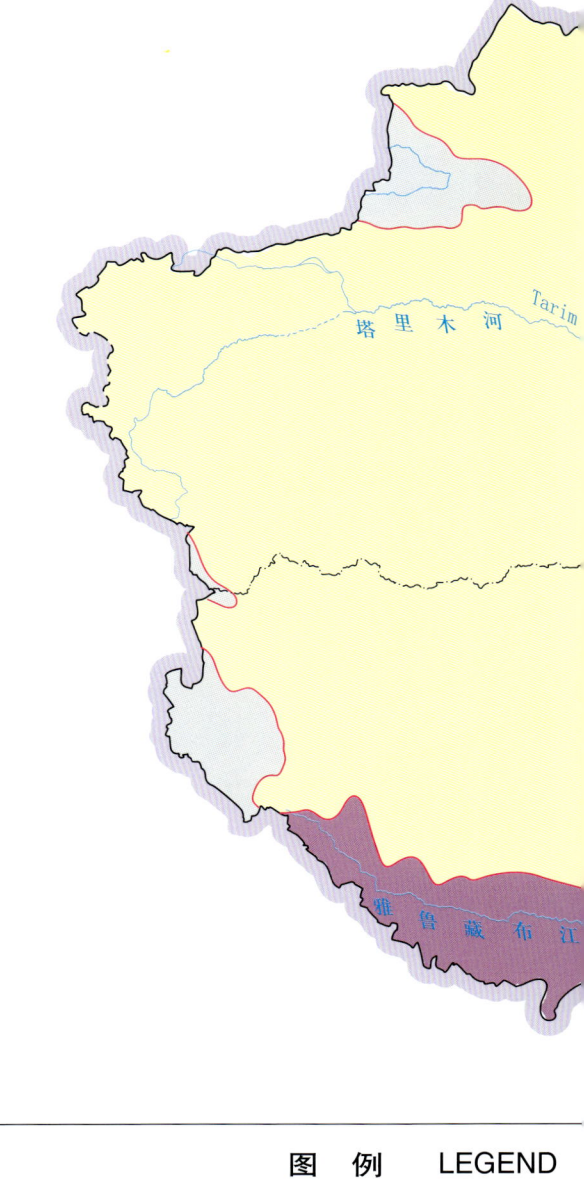

图 例　LEGEND

| | | | |
|---|---|---|---|
| 1 | 黑龙江流域 Heilong River Basin | 7 | 长江流域 Yangtze River Basin |
| 2 | 辽河流域 Liaohe River Basin | 8 | 东南沿海诸河流域 Southeast River Basin |
| 3 | 滦河流域 Luanhe River Basin | 9 | 珠江流域 Pearl River Basin |
| 4 | 海河流域 Haihe River Basin | 10 | 沅江-红河流域 Yuanjiang River–Honghe River Basin |
| 5 | 黄河流域 Yellow River Basin | 11 | 澜沧江-湄公河流域 Lancang River–Mekong River Basin |
| 6 | 淮河流域 Huaihe River Basin | 12 | 怒江-萨尔温江流域 Nujiang–Thanlwin River Basin |

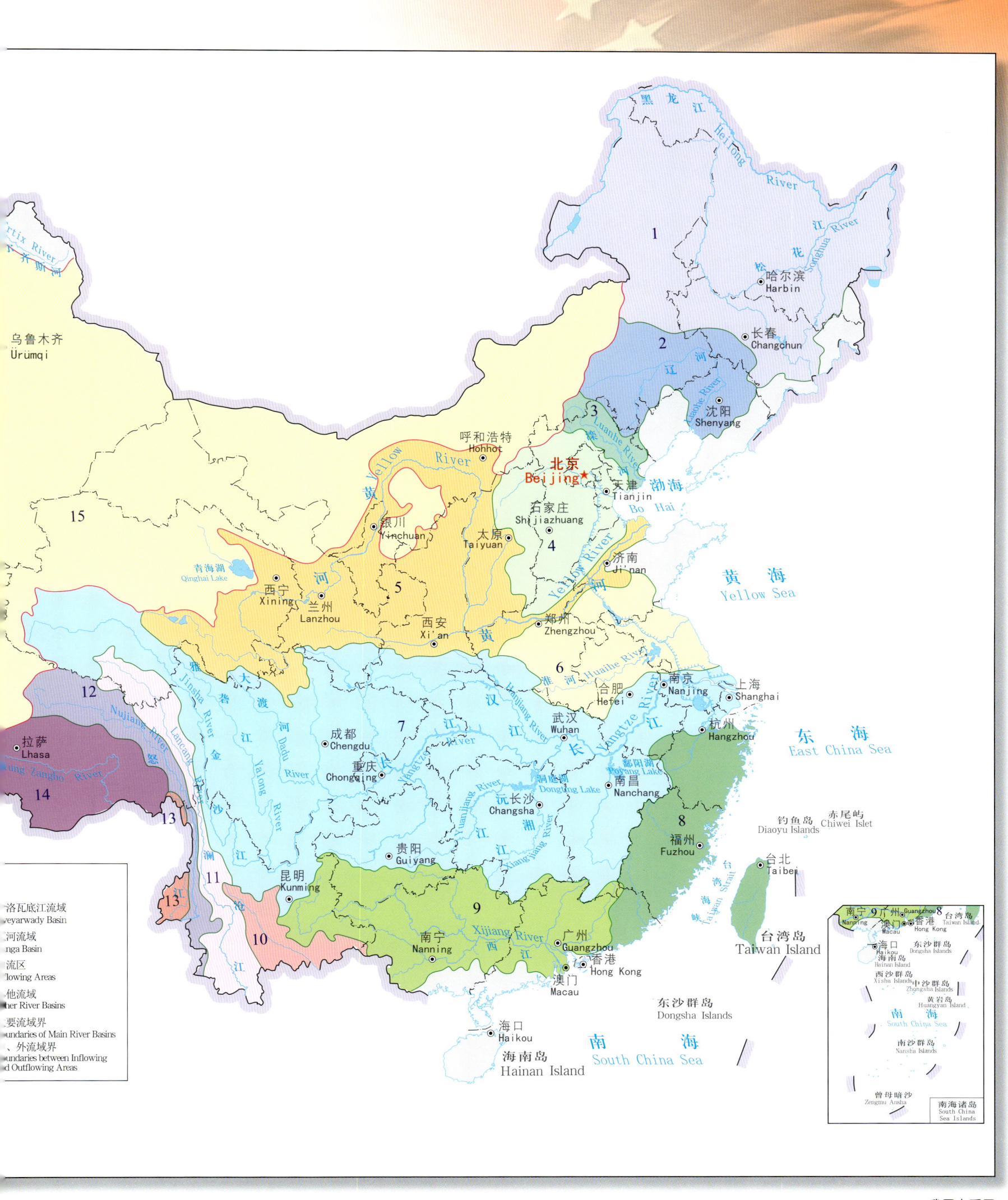

我国水系图
Map of China's River Systems

我国水能资源十分丰富。水能理论总蕴藏量为6.94亿千瓦，理论年发电量为6.08万亿千瓦时；经济可开发装机容量为4.02亿千瓦，经济可开发年发电量为1.75万亿千瓦时。不论是总蕴藏量还是可开发量，均居世界第一位。但水能资源分布很不均衡，主要集中在经济发展相对滞后的西部地区，在经济相对发达的东南部特别是平原地带，水能资源很少。

Having abundant hydro potential, the theoretical potential is 694 million kW, and the theoretical annual generation is 6,080 billion kW·h. The installed capacity which can be economically developed is 402 million kW, and the annul amount of power generation which can be economically developed is 1,750 billion kW·h. The total hydro potential and the amount of power generation which can be developed both rank the 1st in the world. However, hydro resources are unevenly distributed in space and mainly located in the poverty-stricken west area, which does not match the outlay of China's economic development.

**装机容量（总规模）：283724 MW**
**Install capacity(Total Scale): 283724**

◆ 统计口径为大中型电站（装机容量50 MW及以上
Statistics are from large and medium-sized power stations(Install capacity 50 MW and plus)

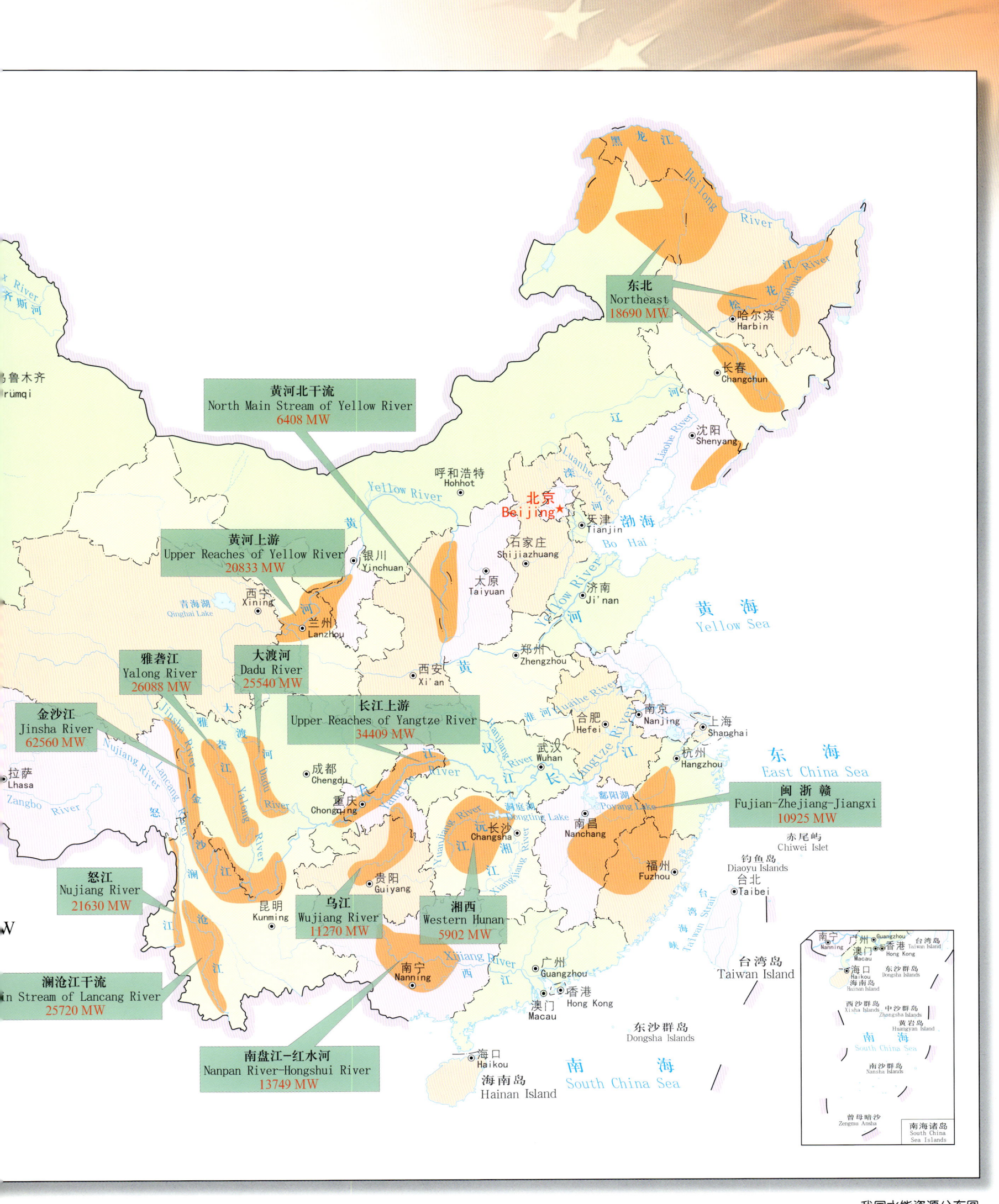

我国水能资源分布图
The Distribution Map of China's Hydropower Potentials

我国有丰富的冰川资源。冰川总面积为58650平方千米，主要分布在西部的6个省份，其中西藏、新疆两个自治区的冰川面积约占全国的90%。冰川储水总量约为51320亿立方米，年平均冰川融水量约为563亿立方米。

China has rich glacier resources. The total area of glacier is 58,650 km². The glacier mainly locates in the 6 provinces and autonomous regions in the west, among which 90% is in Tibet Autonomous Region and Xinjiang Uygur Autonomous Region. Total water stored by glacier is about 5,132 billion m³ and average annual melt water is 56.3 billion m³.

Chapter I Natural Conditions and History 第一篇 自然与历史

① 长江源头冰川
Glacier at the source of the Yangtze River

② 西藏卡若拉冰川
Kharola Glacier in Tibet Autonomous Region

长江——我国第一大河、世界第三大河，干流自西向东流经11个省（自治区、直辖市），流域涉及19个省（自治区、直辖市），面积180万平方千米，干流全长6397千米

The Yangtze River, the largest river in China and the 3rd in the world, flows through 11 provinces, autonomous regions and municipalities from west to east, and the river basin covers 19 provinces, autonomous regions and municipalities with total basin area of 1.8 million km² and the total length reaches 6,397 km

Chapter I Natural Conditions and History 第一篇 自然与历史

黄河——世界著名的多泥沙河流，在我国北部自西向东流经9个省（自治区），流域面积79.5万平方千米，干流全长5464千米

The Yellow River, world renowned river with heavy sedimentation, flows through 9 provinces and autonomous regions from west to east with a total basin area of 0.795 million km² and the total length reaches 5,464 km

淮河——流域面积27万平方千米，干流全长1000千米，由淮河及沂沭泗河两个水系组成
The Huaihe River, with a total catchment of 270 thousand km², and a main stream length of 1,000 km, is composed by the Huaihe River and the Yishusihe River Systems

Chapter I  Natural Conditions and History 第一篇 自然与历史

海河——流域面积32.06万平方千米，由海河、徒骇马颊河、滦河三个水系组成，海河干流加一级支流全长1787千米，徒骇马颊河全长845千米，滦河全长888千米

The Haihe River. The total catchment of Haihe River is 320.6 thousand km², and is composed by Haihe River, Tuhaimajia River and Luanhe River. The length of the Haihe River is 1,787 km, Tuhaimajia River is 845 km and Luanhe River is 888 km

Chapter I　Natural Conditions and History　第一篇　自然与历史

珠江——流域面积45.37万平方千米（其中我国境内44.25万平方千米，其余在越南境内），干流全长2214千米，由西江、北江、东江及珠江三角洲诸河四个水系组成

The Pearl River. The total catchment of the Pearl River is 453.7 thousand km$^2$ (442.5 thousand km$^2$ is located in China, and the rest in Vietnam). The length of main stream is 2,214 km. Its river basin is composed by Xijiang, Beijiang, Dongjiang and several other river systems in the delta

松花江——流域面积18.93万平方千米，干流全长939千米，其北源是嫩江，南源是第二松花江

The Songhua River. The total catchment of the Songhua River is 189.3 thousand km², and the length of its main stream is 939 km. Its north source is Nenjiang River and its south source is the Second Songhua River

辽河——流域面积19.37万平方千米，干流全长1345千米
The Liaohe River. The total catchment of the Liaohe River is 193.7 thousand km², and the length of its main stream is 1,345 km

Chapter I  Natural Conditions and History 第一篇 自然与历史

我国湖泊星罗棋布。湖水面积在1.0平方千米以上的湖泊有2943个，湖泊总面积约为8.45万平方千米，其中面积大于10平方千米的湖泊639个，总面积7.76万平方千米，占1.0平方千米以上湖泊总面积的91.8%，储水总量为7432亿立方米，其中淡水储量约为2250亿立方米。众多湖泊或明媚玉洁，或幽深蜿蜒。鄱阳湖、洞庭湖、太湖、洪泽湖和巢湖五大淡水湖自古即为鱼米之乡。青海湖位于青海高原，是我国最大的咸水湖。

There are thousands of lakes in China. 2943 lakes have a lake area of exceeding 1 km$^2$ with a total lake area of 84,500 km$^2$. 639 lakes have a lake area over 10 km$^2$ with a total lake area of 77,600 km$^2$, accounting for 91.8% of the total lake areas. The total lake storage capacity is 743.2 billion m$^3$, in which freshwater is 225 billion m$^3$. The lakes have diversified features, either in brightness and cleanness or deepness and zigzag. Poyang Lake, Dongting Lake, Taihu Lake, Hongze Lake and Chaohu Lake are five major freshwater lakes. Qinghai Lake is located in the Qinghai Plateau, the largest saltwater lake in China.

① 鄱阳湖——我国第一大淡水湖，水域面积约3914平方千米，位于江西省
The Poyang Lake. Located in Jiangxi Province, Poyang Lake is the largest freshwater lake with a catchment area of 3,914 km$^2$

② 洞庭湖——我国第二大淡水湖，水域面积约2625平方千米，位于湖南省
The Dongting Lake. Situated in Hunan Province, Dongting Lake is the 2nd largest freshwater lake in China with a catchment area of 2,625 km$^2$

③ 太湖——我国第三大淡水湖，水域面积约2338平方千米，位于江苏省与浙江省交界处
The Taihu Lake. Situated on the border of Jiangsu Province and Zhejiang Province, Taihu Lake is the 3rd largest freshwater lake in China with a catchment area of 2,338 km$^2$

Chapter I Natural Conditions and History 第一篇 自然与历史

27

① 洪泽湖——我国第四大淡水湖，水域面积约1597平方千米，位于江苏省
The Hongze Lake. Located in Jinagsu Province, Hongze Lake is the 4th largest freshwater lake in China with a catchment area of 1,597 km$^2$

② 巢湖——我国第五大淡水湖，水域面积约750平方千米，位于安徽省
The Chaohu Lake. Located in Anhui Province, Chaohu Lake is the 5th largest freshwater lake in China with a catchment area of 750 km$^2$

Chapter I Natural Conditions and History 第一篇 自然与历史

③ 长白山天池——第二松花江、图们江、鸭绿江三江之源，是我国和朝鲜的界湖，湖的北部在吉林省境内，水域面积约9.82平方千米
The Tianchi Lake in Changbai Mountain, the source of the Tumen River, Yalu River and Second Songhua River, is a boundary lake between China and DPRK. The north part of the lake is located in Jilin Province with an area of 9.82 km$^2$

④ 千岛湖——新安江水电站大坝蓄水形成的人工湖，水域面积约573平方千米，位于浙江省
The Qiandao Lake, an artificial lake formed after the construction of Xin'anjiang Hydropower Station, is located in Zhejiang Province. The catchment area is about 573 km$^2$

⑤ 青海湖——我国最大的咸水湖，水域面积约4282平方千米，位于青海省
The Qinghai Lake, the largest salt water lake in China, is located in Qinghai Province, with a total catchment area of 4,282 km$^2$

29

我国水资源独特的时空分布，造就了绚丽多彩的自然风光。水作为景观形态，有相对静谧的湖与潭，也有不停流动的江与瀑。波涛汹涌、飞扬激荡的江河显示了水的动态之美；而烟波浩淼、一碧万顷的湖泊则表现了水的静态之美。长江三峡、黄河壶口瀑布、桂林山水、杭州西湖、四川九寨沟、贵州黄果树瀑布、钱塘江涌潮等，都是闻名世界的自然胜景。

The unique time and space distribution of water resources create marvelous natural views in China. As a landscape pattern, water can be formed into serene lakes and pool, or running rivers and waterfalls. Rivers with waves surging turbulently reveal the dynamic beauty of water, whereas lakes with blue water reaching far beyond the horizon display the static beauty of water. The Three Gorges of the Yangtze River, Hukou Waterfall on the Yellow River, Landscape in Guilin City, West Lake in Hangzhou City, Jiuzhaigou in Sichuan Province, Huangguoshu Waterfalls in Guizhou Province, tidal bore in Qiantang River, etc., are all world-known tourist attractions.

长江三峡风光

Three Gorges of the Yangtze River

Chapter I Natural Conditions and History 第一篇 自然与历史

黄河壶口瀑布
Hukou Waterfall on the Yellow River

四川九寨沟
Jiuzhaigou in Sichuan Province

# 兴利除害 富国惠民 —— 新中国水利60年
Generate Benefits and Mitigate Hazards to Contribute to the Prosperity of the Nation and the Interests of the People
—— 60 Years' Water Development in China

① 杭州西湖
West Lake in Hangzhou City

② 桂林山水
Landscape in Guilin City

③ 武汉东湖
East Lake in Wuhan City

Chapter I  Natural Conditions and History  第一篇  自然与历史

③

① 贵州黄果树瀑布
   Huangguoshu Waterfalls in Guizhou Province

② 广西德天瀑布
   Detian Waterfalls, Guangxi Zhuang Autonomous Region

Chapter I  Natural Conditions and History 第一篇 自然与历史

## ◆ 治水历史
## History of Water Management

我国自古就是一个水旱灾害频繁发生的国家。据不完全统计，从公元前206年到1949年的2155年间，我国发生较大的水灾1092次，较大旱灾1056次，也就是几乎每年都有一次较大的水灾或旱灾，其中尤以黄淮海平原和长江中下游最为严重。除水害、兴水利是历朝历代治国安邦的大事。传说中的大禹治水，李冰父子修建举世闻名的都江堰，可与长城媲美的全长1700千米的京杭大运河等，都说明了治水的重大战略意义。水利兴则国泰民安，水利衰则社会动荡，这就是中国历史的见证。一部辉煌的中国历史，可以说，也是一部可歌可泣的治水史。我国是水利大国、水利古国，几千年的治水实践积累了丰富的经验。我国古代的治水活动及其成就，主要集中在农田水利、内河航运和防洪治河三个领域。

China has been hitting by frequent flooding and drought disasters since ancient times. According to incomplete statistics, during the 2,155 years from 206 BC to 1949, China witnessed 1,092 floods and 1,056 droughts, both of relatively big scale. Almost every year, China, particularly Huang-Huai-Hai Plain and middle and lower reaches of the Yangtze River, experienced an occurrence of flood or drought. Preventing water disasters and constructing water projects has always been one of the essential tasks in all dynasties. The legend of Dayu, the Dujiangyan Weir built by Li Bing family, and the 1,700 km Grand Canal which is comparable with the Great Wall have demonstrated the strategic significance and importance of water management. History tells us that water conservancy brings benefits to the people and the country, and neglecting water management results in social instability. The glamorous history of China is, in some sense, a grand history of water management. China has generated rich experiences through thousands of years' water management practice. The ancient water conservancy and management mainly focus on three areas: farmland infrastructure, river navigation, river training and flood prevention.

Chapter I Natural Conditions and History 第一篇 自然与历史

都江堰鱼嘴、宝瓶口、飞沙堰
Yuzui (fish mouth), Feisha Weir, Bottle Mouth of Dujiangyan Weir

都江堰渠首及李冰治水六字诀
Headworks of Dujiangyan Weir and six-character water management guidance proposed by Mr. Li Bing

我国在西周时期（公元前1046—前771）便出现了系统的农田灌溉排水设施。春秋时代（前770—前476），楚国建成了大型灌溉工程——期思陂和芍陂，后者经过改造成了当代淠史杭灌区的一个反调节水库（安丰塘）。战国时代（前475—前221），魏国修建了引漳十二渠，因有12条渠道而得名，灌溉了漳河南岸大片农田。秦国兴建的著名灌溉工程都江堰和以主要建设者姓名命名的郑国渠，分别拥有300万亩（15亩＝1公顷，下同）和195万亩的灌溉面积，为秦国统一天下奠定了强大的物质基础。相传西汉时期，今新疆地区创建了奇特的地下灌溉工程坎儿井，一直沿用至今。

春秋时，吴国开凿了扬州至淮安的运河——邗沟，沟通了长江与淮河水系。战国时，魏国开凿中牟至开封的运河——鸿沟，沟通了黄淮水系。秦代（前221—前206），人们又在今广西兴安县开凿了灵渠，沟通了珠江与长江水系。自此，形成了沟通全国的水运交通网络。隋朝（581—618）时，先是开凿了通济渠，沟通了洛阳到扬州的水上交通线；随后又开凿了永济渠，沟通了洛阳到今北京的水上交通线。以洛阳为中心、南达扬州、北到北京的水上运输动脉基本建成。到了元代（1206—1368），著名的南北向的京杭大运河开通，将政治中心北京与经济中心江南地区连为一体。这条大动脉直到清末甚至现代都在发挥作用，为国家的稳定繁荣作出了重大贡献。

China developed systematic irrigation and drainage facilities in West Zhou Dynasty (1046 BC–771 BC). In Spring and Autumn Period (770 BC–476 BC), Chu State built two large scale irrigation projects: Qisi Reservoir and Quebei Reservoir, and the latter was later developed into a regulating reservoir (Anfeng Reservoir) in Pishihang Irrigation District. In Warring State Period (475 BC–221 BC), Wei State constructed 12 canals to divert water from Zhanghe River to the farmland on the river's south bank. Qin State built the world famous Dujiangyan Weir and Zhengguo Canal (named after the builder), which can irrigate areas of 3 million *mu* (15 *mu* = 1 hectare) and 1.95 million *mu* respectively. These projects laid a solid foundation for Qin State conquering and uniting the rest of China. It was said that in West Han Dynasty, local residents invented the miracle underground irrigation system of Karez Well in Xinjiang, which is still in operation nowadays.

In Spring and Autumn Period, Wu State built the Hangou Canal from Yangzhou to Huai'an, linking Yangtze River and Huaihe River. In Warring States Period, Wei State constructed Honggou Canal from Zhongmu to Kaifeng, linking the Yellow River and Huaihe River. In Qin Dynasty (221 BC–206 BC), people dug Lingqu Canal in Xing'an County, Guangxi Zhuang Autonomous Region, linking the Pearl River and the Yangtze River. Since then, a country-wide river navigation and transportation network was formed. In Sui Dynasty (581–618), Tongji Canal was dug, linking Luoyang and Yangzhou. A Yongji Canal was later constructed to link Luoyang and Beijing. A river transportation network that centered Luoyang, and reached Yangzhou in the south and Beijing in the north was established. In Yuan Dynasty (1206–1368), the famous Grand Canal was constructed and put into use, linking the political capital Beijing with economic center of China. Till today, the Grand Canal is still serving the stability and prosperity of the country.

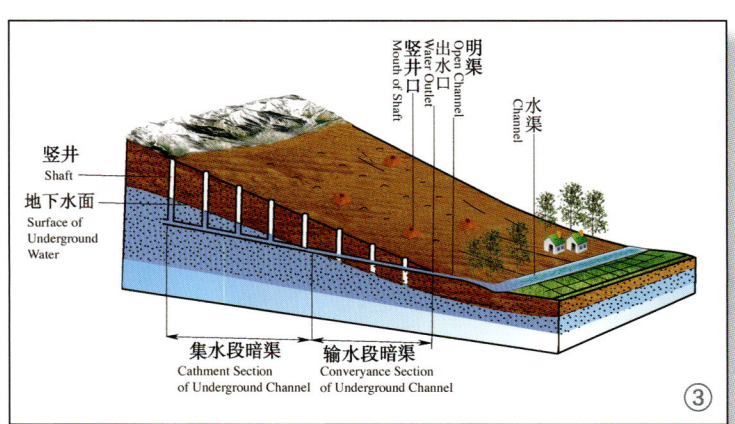

① 郑国渠今貌
　Remains of Zhengguo Canal

② 芍陂今貌（安丰塘）
　Remains of Quebei (Anfeng Reservoir)

③ 坎儿井示意图
　Diagram of Karez Well

④ 现代坎儿井
　Modern Karez Well

⑤ 灵渠渠首今貌
　Remains of Inlet of Lingqu Canal

传说公元前 21 世纪，黄河流域发生持续性大洪水，大禹采用疏导的办法，历时 13 年将洪水排入大海。西汉（公元前 207—公元 25）时，黄河在瓠子决口，汉武帝亲临指挥堵口成功。西汉末年，黄河决溢漫流七八十年，王景治河成功，号称"三年两决口、百年一改道"的黄河自此维持了七八百年未改道。东汉时，东南沿海开始兴修海塘工程。到了明代（1368—1644），潘季驯提出了"束水攻沙"的治河主张，采取遥堤、缕堤、格堤、月堤等系统的堤防工程措施加大河水挟沙能力，使黄河治理的理念与实践达到了空前高度。

In the 21st century BC, the Yellow River Basin was struck by constant long lasting large floods. Dayu employed the method of diversion, and it took him 13 years to empty the flood water into sea. In West Han Dynasty (207 BC-25 AD), the Yellow River breached at Huzi, King Hanwu showed up on the scene and successfully blocked the breach point. In the last few years of West Han Dynasty, frequent over-toppings were seen along the Yellow River. Wang Jing, a water official, successfully controlled Yellow River which was known for "2 inrushes within 3 years and route changes within 100 years", maintained its original river route for 700-800 years. In East Han Dynasty, sea walls were constructed in southeastern coastal area. In Ming Dynasty (1368-1644), Pan Jixun forwarded the idea of "allocating water to scour sand", and built systemic dikes, including Yaodi dike, Loudi dike, Gedi dike, Yuedi dike, etc., to increase the sand-carrying capacity of the Yellow River, highly enriched the Yellow River Management theory and practice.

Chapter I  Natural Conditions and History　第一篇　自然与历史

① 京杭大运河船队
　Fleets in the Grand Canal
② 河南郑州市黄河滩区的大禹治水像
　The Statue of Dayu, in flood plain in Zhengzhou City, Henan Province
③ 潘季驯《河防一览》图（著于1590年，明代）
　"An Overview of Flood Defense Works" by Pan Jixun (written in 1590, Ming Dynasty)

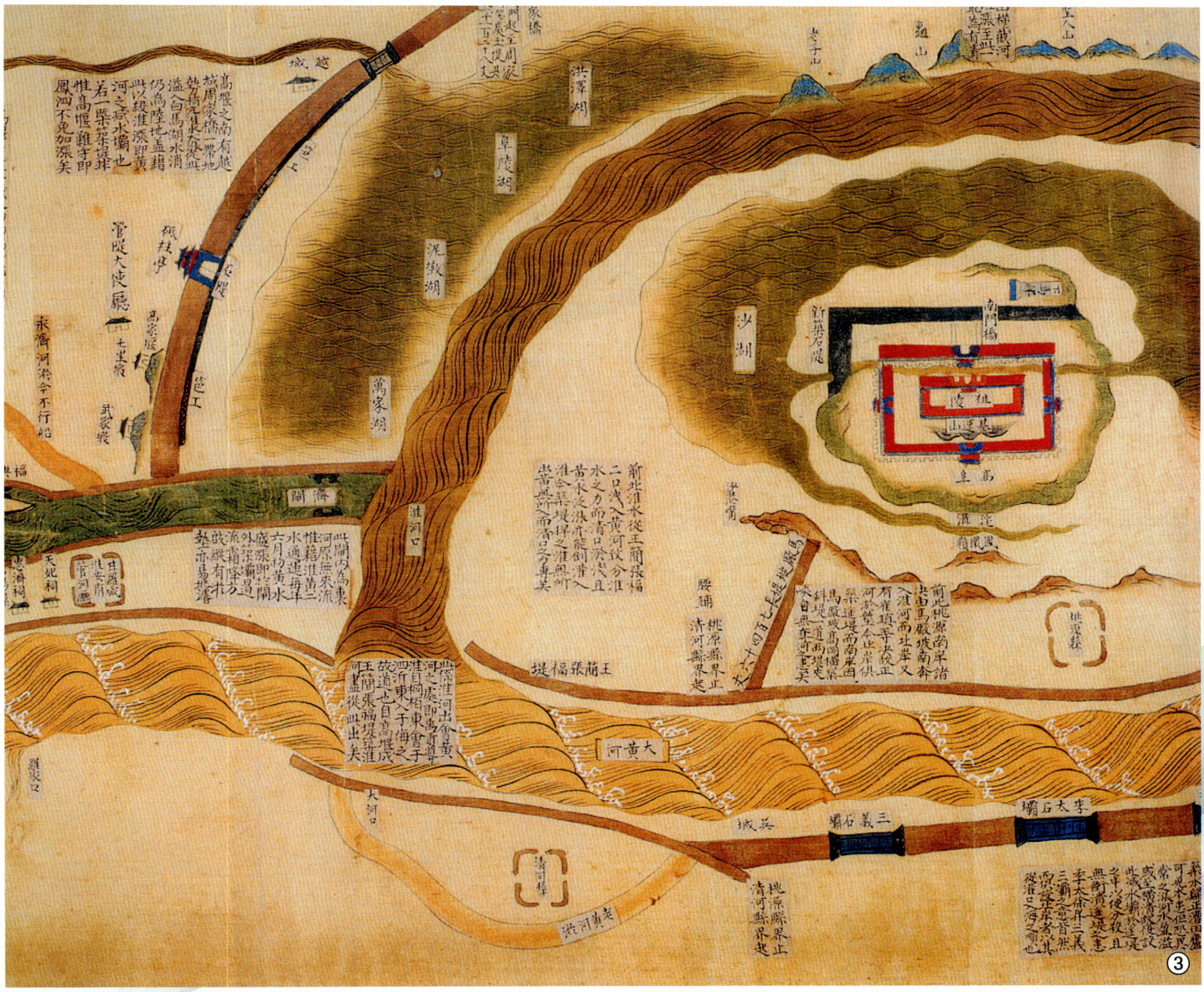

几千年来的封建统治，使中华民族苦难深重。进入20世纪，中国人民虽然推翻了封建的清王朝，但在半封建半殖民地的旧中国，由于外侮深重、军阀混战、水利失修、科学技术停滞不前，水利建设一蹶不振，水政混乱，水旱灾害频繁，民不聊生。在新中国成立以前，水利设施可以说廖廖无几，中国人民处在水深火热之中。

The Chinese nation has suffered thousands of years of feudal society. Though the Chinese people overthrew the Qing Dynasty in the beginning of the 20th century, China, a semi-colonial and semi-feudal society, was suffering from civil wars by warlords. Due to in-depth foreign intervention and constant fights among warlords, water facilities was not repaired and maintained. Flood and drought disasters occurred frequently and people can't live in peace. Till 1949, few water projects had survived and the Chinese people were living in extreme misery.

① 1915年广州水灾
Flood in Guangzhou City in 1915

② 1917年海河大水天津灾民流离失所
People lost home during the Haihe River flood in Tianjin City in 1917

③ 1931年武汉水灾
Flood in Wuhan City in 1931

④ 1938年国民党军队掘开黄河花园口，造成黄河泛滥，千百万人无家可归
Thousands of people lost home when Kuomintang troops blasted the Yellow River at Huayuankou in 1938

只有社会主义才能救中国。1949年新中国成立以后,党和政府始终高度重视水利工作,把治水作为安民兴邦的大事来抓,采取了一系列促进水利发展的重大政策措施。领导全国人民大规模治理江河,开发水资源,发展农田灌溉、城乡供水、水力发电,治理水土流失,加强水资源节约保护和水生态环境保护,有力地推动了水利事业的快速发展。在波澜壮阔的治水实践中,华夏儿女众志成城,艰苦创业,治山治水,除害兴利,涌现了无数英杰,凝聚了民族力量,体现了社会主义制度的优越性,铸就了"献身、负责、求实"的水利行业精神。水利为保障人民群众生命财产安全、国民经济平稳较快发展、人民生活水平提高作出了重大贡献,在新中国成立60年的历史上谱写了光辉的篇章。

Since the founding of the People's Republic of China in 1949, the Chinese government has always attached great attention to water management, and undertook strategic policies and measures to promote water management and development in farmland irrigation, urban and rural water supply, hydropower generation, soil and water conservation, and ecological and environmental protection. Chinese people join hands and make concerted effort in water disaster prevention and water management. "Sacrifice, responsibility and truth-seeking" has become profession spirit in water sector. Water management has made remarkable devotion to safeguarding the lives and property of the general public, stable and rapid development of the national economy, and the improvement of people's lives. A glamorous chapter is written in the 60-year history of the People's Republic of China.

# 第二篇　建设与成就

新中国成立60年来，水利的重要地位和作用日益为全社会所认识，国家明确水利是国民经济和社会发展的基础设施，水利事业由主要为农业服务向为国民经济和社会发展全面服务转变，水利投入大幅度增加，水利建设大规模展开，水利保障经济社会发展的能力和水平实现跨越式提升。

截至2008年底，全国共完成水利固定资产投资达10034.63亿元，建成各类水库8.64万座，水库总库容6924亿立方米，堤防总长度28.7万千米，发展农田有效灌溉面积8.77亿亩，水电装机容量达到1.72亿千瓦，初步形成了防洪、排涝、灌溉、供水、发电等水利工程体系，极大地改善了我国大江大河大湖的防洪状况，优化了全国水资源配置格局，增强了水利对经济社会发展的保障能力。

# Chapter II
# Construction and Achievements

Since 1949, the importance of water management has been recognized by the whole society. Chinese government has defined that water infrastructure is the foundation for socio-economic development. Water conservancy and water management should not only serve for agriculture, but also expand to other sectors of national economy. With increased investment in water sector, water construction has been promoted on large scale which in turn better serves socio-economic development.

By the end of 2008, China has invested over 1,003.463 billion *Yuan* in fixed assets in water sector, building 86,400 reservoirs with a total storage capacity of 692.4 billion $m^3$. Irrigated area has totalled 877 million *mu* and hydropower installed capacity has reached 172 million kW. A water project system that covers flood prevention, drainage, irrigation, water supply and power generation has greatly improved flood prevention on major rivers and lakes, rationalized national water allocation, and enhanced the supporting role of water to socio-economic development.

## ◆ 大江大河治理
## Harnessing and Training of Major Rivers and Lakes

新中国成立60年来，党和政府始终高度重视大江大河的治理，坚持"蓄泄兼筹、以泄为主"的防洪方针，加固堤防，建设干支流控制工程，开展蓄滞洪区安全建设，进行病险水库除险加固，清淤除障，疏浚河湖。1998年大水后，党中央作出了灾后重建、整治江湖、兴修水利的重大战略部署，加强江河堤防建设，有计划有步骤地开展平垸行洪、退田还湖、移民建镇，开展水土保持，加强防洪非工程措施建设，在大江大河的治理上取得了显著成就。目前，长江中下游干堤已经修完修好，黄河下游标准化堤防建设全面展开，治淮、治太骨干工程基本完成，三峡、小浪底、临淮岗等枢纽工程全面发挥效益。我国大江大河主要河段基本具备防御新中国成立以来发生的最大洪水的能力，中小河流具备防御一般洪水的能力，重点海堤设防标准提高到50年一遇。

Since 1949, the Chinese government has always attached great importance to the harnessing and training of major rivers and lakes, scrupulously abide by the guideline of "coordination of floodwater storage and discharge, and discharge comes the first", reinforced dikes, built controlling projects, constructed flood storage and detention areas, strengthened risky reservoirs, and dredged rivers and lakes. After the big flood in 1998, the Chinese government made the plan on reconstruction, river and lake harnessing and training and projects construction, enhanced dike construction, returned the farmland to lakes, built new home for the relocatees, and implemented non-structural measures. Remarkable achievements have been witnessed after the above-mentioned measures have been undertaken. At present, dikes along the middle and lower reaches of the Yangtze River have been completed. Standard dikes are under construction along the Yellow River, key projects addressing problems of the Huaihe River and Taihu Lake have been completed, and Three Gorges Project, Xiaolangdi Project and Linhuaigang Project have generated benefits. Main sections along major rivers and lakes can withstand the biggest flood ever occurred after 1949, small and medium-sized rivers can defend ordinary flood, while key coastal levees can hold flood with an occurrence of 50 years.

我国重要水库、水利枢纽和堤防分布图
Map of the Layout of Major Reservoirs, Water Projects and Dikes

# 兴利除害 富国惠民 —— 新中国水利60年

**Generate Benefits and Mitigate Hazards to Contribute to the Prosperity of the Nation and the Interests of the People**
—— 60 Years' Water Development in China

① 葛洲坝水利枢纽——长江上修建的第一个大坝，是三峡水利枢纽的重要组成部分。电站总装机容量271.5万千瓦
Gezhouba Water Project, the first one built on the Yangtze River, is an important component of the Three Gorges Project. The installed capacity is 2.715 million kW

Chapter II Construction and Achievements  第二篇  建设与成就

② 长江三峡水利枢纽——当今世界上最大的水利枢纽工程，防洪库容221.5亿立方米，可使下游荆江大堤的防洪能力由过去防御10年一遇的洪水提高到抵御100年一遇的洪水。电站总装机容量2250万千瓦

The Three Gorges Project, the largest water project in the world and the key project managing and developing the Yangtze River, its storage capacity is 22.15 billion m³ and installed capacity is 22.50 million kW. The project has raised the flood defense capacity of Jingjiang Dike from 10-year occurrence to 100-year occurrence

③ 1997年11月6日长江三峡工程进行大江截流

Closure of the Yangtze River at the Three Gorges Project on November 6, 1997

# 60

**兴利除害 富国惠民** —— 新中国水利60年

Generate Benefits and Mitigate Hazards to Contribute to the Prosperity of the Nation and the Interests of the People
—— 60 Years' Water Development in China

① 整治前的湖北汉阳南岸嘴
Nan'anzui, in Wuhan City, Hubei Province, before reinforcement

② 整治后的湖北汉阳南岸嘴
Nan'anzui, in Wuhan City, Hubei Province, after reinforcement

③ 湖北丹江口水利枢纽——有效控制了汉江（长江最大支流）上游的洪水，水库总库容290.5亿立方米，电站总装机容量90万千瓦
The Danjiangkou Reservoir. It has effectively defended the flood from upper-reaches of Hanjiang River, the largest tributary of Yangtze River. The storage capacity is 29.05 billion m$^3$ and the installed capacity is 0.9 million kW

④ 湖南岳阳长江干堤加固工程
Reinforced dike along mainstream of the Yangtze River, Yueyang City, Hunan Province

⑤ 整修加固后的长江大堤
The Yangtze River dikes after reinforcement

Chapter II Construction and Achievements 第二篇 建设与成就

① 1997年10月黄河小浪底工程进行截流
Closure of the Yellow River at the Xiaolangdi Water Project in October 1997

② 黄河小浪底水利枢纽——治理开发黄河的关键性工程，可有效控制黄河洪水，使黄河下游花园口的防洪标准由60年一遇提高到1000年一遇，水库总库容126.5亿立方米，电站总装机容量180万千瓦
Xiaolangdi Water Project, a key project in the management and development of the Yellow River, has effectively controlled flood and raised the flood defense capacity at Huayuankou from 60-year occurrence to 1000-year occurrence. The storage capacity is 12.65 billion m³, and installed capacity is 1.8 million kW

# 兴利除害 富国惠民 —— 新中国水利60年
## Generate Benefits and Mitigate Hazards to Contribute to the Prosperity of the Nation and the Interests of the People
—— 60 Years' Water Development in China

① 黄河三门峡水利枢纽——黄河干流上修建的第一座大型水库，总库容162亿立方米，电站总装机容量40万千瓦
Sanmenxia Water Project, the first large-scale water project built on the mainstream of the Yellow River, has a storage capacity of 16.2 billion m³ and an installed capacity of 0.4 million kW

② 黄河万家寨水利枢纽——我国第一个由中央和地方合作建设的大型水利水电工程，水库总库容8.96亿立方米，电站总装机容量108万千瓦，年供水量可达14亿立方米
Wanjiazhai Water Project, the first large-scale water project co-constructed by the central government and local government has a storage capacity of 896 million m³ and an installed capacity of 1.08 million kW. The annual water supply capacity has reached 1.4 billion m³

③ 黄河堤防工程——保护黄淮海平原的生命线
The Yellow River dike project is the lifeline for Huang-Huai-Hai Plain

# 兴利除害 富国惠民 —— 新中国水利60年
## Generate Benefits and Mitigate Hazards to Contribute to the Prosperity of the Nation and the Interests of the People
### —— 60 Years' Water Development in China

① 新沂河入海水道海口控制工程——增加淮河入海出路的一条分洪道

The Controlling project at the river mouth of Xinyi River serves as a flood diversion channel of the Huaihe River

② 姜唐湖进洪闸——临淮岗洪水控制工程主要建筑物之一，参与分泄淮河干流洪水

The flood gate of Jiangtang Lake, a key compartment of Linhuaigang Project, can divert and discharge flood in the mainstream of the Huaihe River

③ 淮河入海水道——扩大淮河洪水出路，提高洪泽湖防洪标准，确保淮河下游地区防洪安全的战略性骨干工程

The Huaihe River flowing into sea. The project has expanded the flood flow channel, raised flood defense capacity of Hongze Lake and ensured the safety of the lower reaches area

④ 佛子岭水库——淮河流域的大型山谷水库，总库容4.96亿立方米，可有效减轻淮河中下游洪水负担

The Foziling Reservoir, a large-scale reservoir in the valley of the Huaihe River, has effectively alleviated the flood defense burden on the middle and lower reaches of the Huaihe River. The storage capacity is 496 million m$^3$

⑤ 淮河流域临淮岗洪水控制工程。该工程结束了淮河中游无防洪控制性工程的历史

The Linhuaigang Flood Control Project on the Huaihe River, the first project of its kind on the middle reaches of the Huaihe River

⑥ 淮河淮北大堤——淮河中游防洪体系中保护面积最大的主要堤防

The Huaibei Dike on the Huaihe River is a major dike in the flood defense system of the middle reaches of the Huaihe River, protecting the widest area

Chapter II  Construction and Achievements　第二篇　建设与成就

① 官厅水库——新中国成立后建设的第一座大型水库
  Guanting Reservoir, the first large-scale reservoir constructed after 1949

② 20世纪60年代开挖的子牙新河,用于分泄子牙河上游洪水,减轻海河洪水入海负担
  Ziya (New) River dug in the 1960s to discharge flood from upper reaches of the Ziya River and reduce the burden on the Haihe River

③ 海河尾闾的海河防潮闸
  The tide gate of the Haihe River Estuary

④ 保障河北石家庄市防洪安全的黄壁庄水库
  Huangbizhuang Reservoir to defend flood and safeguard Shijiazhuang City, Hebei Province

Chapter II Construction and Achievements 第二篇 建设与成就

# 60

**兴利除害 富国惠民** —— 新中国水利60年

Generate Benefits and Mitigate Hazards to Contribute to the Prosperity of the Nation and the Interests of the People
— 60 Years' Water Development in China

① 飞来峡水利枢纽——广东北江流域综合治理的关键工程，防洪库容13.36亿立方米，可使北江大堤防御300年一遇的洪水
   Feilaixia Water Project, a key project in the comprehensive management of the Beijiang River in Guangdong Province, has a storage capacity of 1.336 billion m³ and raises the flood defense capacity of Beijiang River dike to 300-year occurrence

② 百色水利枢纽——珠江流域治理和开发郁江的大型骨干水利工程，水库总库容56.6亿立方米
   Baise Water Project, a large-scale project for the management and development of Yujiang River as stated in the Comprehensive Utilization Planning of Pearl River. The storage capacity is 5.66 billion m³

③ 广州珠江防洪工程
   Flood defense project of the Pearl River, Guangzhou City, Guangdong Province

④ 广西南宁市江北堤
   Jiangbei Dike, Nanning City, Guangxi Zhuang Autonomous Region

Chapter II  Construction and Achievements　第二篇　建设与成就

# 兴利除害 富国惠民 ——新中国水利60年
## Generate Benefits and Mitigate Hazards to Contribute to the Prosperity of the Nation and the Interests of the People
### —— 60 Years' Water Development in China

① 保护黑龙江省哈尔滨市防洪安全的松花江干堤
The Songhua River Dike, protecting Harbin City, Heilongjiang Province

② 嫩江堤防
Nenjiang River Dike

③ 尼尔基水利枢纽——嫩江流域防治水旱灾害的控制性工程，水库总库容86.11亿立方米，可使齐齐哈尔市的防洪标准提高到100年一遇
Nierji Water Project, a controlling project in the Nenjiang River Basin, has a storage capacity of 8.611 billion m³ and raises the flood defense capacity of Qiqihar City to 100-year occurrence

④ 石佛寺水利枢纽——辽河干流唯一的大型控制性水利工程，水库总库容1.85亿立方米，与支流水库及区间堤防组成辽河干流防洪体系，可使下游防洪标准提高到100年一遇
Shifosi Water Project, the only large-scale controlling project on the mainstream of Liaohe River, has a storage capacity of 185 million m³ and raises the downstream flood defense capacity to 100-year occurrence

⑤ 白石水库——大凌河干流上的大型水利枢纽工程，总库容16.45亿立方米
Baishi Reservoir, a large-scale project on the mainstream of Daling River, has a storage capacity of 1.645 billion m³

⑥ 察尔森水库——嫩江右岸洮儿河干流上唯一的控制性工程，总库容12.53亿立方米
Chaersen Reservoir, the only controlling project on the mainstream of Tao'er River, on the right bank of the Nenjiang River, has a storage capacity of 1.253 billion m³

Chapter II  Construction and Achievements  第二篇  建设与成就

Chapter II Construction and Achievements  第二篇 建设与成就

① 太浦河工程——太湖流域防洪除涝综合治理的骨干工程
　Taipu River Project, a key one for the flood defense of Taihu Lake Basin
② 望虞河工程——解决太湖洪水北排长江问题的重要工程
　Wangyu River Project, a key one to discharge flood from Taihu Lake north to the Yangtze River
③ 南排工程盐官枢纽——可向钱塘江排涝，以减轻太湖流域水涝压力
　Yanguan Complex of Nanpai Project, diverts floodwater to Qiantang River to alleviate burden on the Taihu Lake
④ 望亭水利枢纽——太湖流域防洪、排涝及向太湖调水的重要枢纽工程
　Wangting Water Project, a key one for flood defense and water diversion of the Taihu Lake

71

① 广西柳州市城市防洪工程
Flood defense project in Liuzhou City, Guangxi Zhuang Autonomous Region

② 江西南昌市城市防洪工程
Flood defense project in Nanchang City, Jiangxi Province

③ 湖北武汉市江滩防洪工程
Flood defense project in Wuhan City, Hubei Province

Chapter II  Construction and Achievements  第二篇  建设与成就

**兴利除害 富国惠民** —— 新中国水利60年
Generate Benefits and Mitigate Hazards to Contribute to the Prosperity of the Nation and the Interests of the People
—— 60 Years' Water Development in China

Chapter II  Construction and Achievements　第二篇　建设与成就

① 福建泉州市晋江下游防洪岸线
   Downstream flood defense project of Jinjiang River, Quanzhou City, Fujian Province
② 河北迁安市滦河城区段生态防洪工程
   Flood defense project of the Luanhe River in Qian'an City, Hebei Province
③ 安徽芜湖市城市防洪工程
   Flood defense project in Wuhu City, Anhui Province
④ 江苏南通市城市防洪工程
   Flood defense project in Nantong City, Jiangsu Province

新中国成立60年来，我国先后建成86000多座水库，其中大型水库529座、中型水库3181座，在防洪、灌溉、发电、城乡供水、航运和水产养殖等方面发挥了巨大作用。这些水库绝大多数建于20世纪50年代末到70年代初，限于当时的技术经济条件，有相当一部分水库存在不同程度的病险问题，不仅效益难以充分发挥，而且成为重大安全隐患。1998年以来，国家投入大量资金用于病险水库除险加固。党的十七届三中全会明确提出，2010年底前完成规划内6240座大中型和重点小型病险水库除险加固任务。这些水库在除险加固完成后，可以大大地提高防洪保安能力和供水保障能力，对经济社会的发展将起到重要的作用。

Since 1949, China has built more than 86,000 reservoirs, among which 529 are large ones and 3,181 are medium-sized ones. These reservoirs have played an instrumental role in flood defense, irrigation, power generation, urban and rural water supply, navigation and aqua-culture. However, since most reservoirs were built from the 1950s to the 1970s, they are now troubled with problems of different degree and pose great risks. Since 1998, Chinese government has put a great deal of investment to reinforce risky reservoirs. The target that "by the end of 2010, 6,240 risky reservoirs should be reinforced" has been set at the Third Plenary Session of the 17th Central Committee of the Chinese Communist Party. Once the target is fulfilled, flood defense and water supply capacity of the reservoirs will be raised and they can better serve socio-economic development.

① 除险加固后的河南白沙水库
　Strengthened Baisha Reservoir in Henan Province
② 除险加固后的辽宁大伙房水库
　Strengthened Dahuofang Reservoir in Liaoning Province

① 除险加固后的湖北漳河水库
　Strengthened Zhanghe Reservoir in Hubei Province
② 除险加固后的浙江青山水库
　Strengthened Qingshan Reservoir in Zhejiang Province
③ 除险加固后的江苏横山水库
　Strengthened Hengshan Reservoir in Jiangsu Province
④ 正在除险加固的宁夏寺口子水库
　Strengthened Sikouzi Reservoir in Ningxia Hui Autonomous Region

①
②

① 除险加固后的安徽佛子岭水库
Strengthened Foziling Reservoir in Anhui Province

② 除险加固后的贵州兴西湖水库
Strengthened Xingxihu Reservoir in Guizhou Province

③ 除险加固后的辽宁参窝水库
Strengthened Shenwo Reservoir in Liaoning Province

## ◆ 城乡供水保障
## Provision of Water Supply for Urban and Rural Areas

新中国成立60年来，党和政府大力发展城乡供水，为城乡经济社会发展提供了基础性保障。在加强水源工程建设的同时，先后建成了引滦入津入唐、引碧入连、引黄济青、引青济秦、珠海澳门供水、东江深圳供水等一大批水资源配置工程，多次实施引黄济津和从山西、河北向北京集中输水，实施珠江压咸补淡应急调度，有效缓解了北京、天津、青岛、深圳、厦门、西安、大连、秦皇岛、澳门、香港等城市和地区供水紧张的局面；有效应对了松花江水污染事件、太湖和巢湖蓝藻暴发事件引发的供水危机。为了解决我国北方地区缺水问题，实施了举世瞩目的南水北调工程，其东线、中线一期工程分别于2002年和2003年正式开工。南水北调工程最终调水规模为年均448亿立方米，其中东线148亿立方米，中线130亿立方米。同时，逐年加大力度解决农村人口饮水困难和饮水安全问题，截至2008年底，累计解决了2.72亿农村人口的饮水困难和1.65亿农村人口的饮水不安全问题，基本结束了我国农村严重缺乏饮用水的历史，全国一半以上的农村人口喝上了自来水。全国水利工程年供水能力由新中国成立初期的1000多亿立方米提高到7491亿立方米，为促进国民经济繁荣和社会发展发挥了巨大作用。

During the past 60 years since the founding of the People's Republic of China, the Chinese government has made great efforts to improve the capability of urban and rural water supply, which has fundamentally guaranteed the social and economic development. While enhancing the construction of water sources projects, a great number of water allocation projects have been completed, such as transfer projects from Luanhe River to Tianjin City and Tangshan City, from Biliu River to Dalian City, from Yellow River to Qingdao City and from Qinglong River to Qinhuangdao City, from Dongjiang River to Shenzhen City and Hong Kong SAR, as well as water supply projects to Zhuhai City and Macau SAR, etc. Besides, water from Yellow River has been transferred to Tianjin City several times, while water from Shanxi Province and Hebei Province has been transferred to ensure the water supply in Beijing City and the Pearl River Emergency Water Transfer Project for Repelling Saltwater Intrusion and Supplementing Freshwater been implemented. All these efforts have not only effectively reduced the water supply pressure in relevant cities and regions, including Beijing City, Tianjin City, Qingdao City, Shenzhen City, Xiamen City, Xi'an City, Dalian City, Qinhuangdao City, Macau SAR, Hong Kong SAR, but also effectively responded to the emergencies triggered by Songhua River water pollution accident as well as Taihu Lake and Chaohu Lake green algae explosion. In order to solve the problem of water shortage in northern China, the well-known South-to-North Water Transfer Project with the ultimate water transfer of 44.8 billion $m^3$ has been implemented, among which the east route 14.8 billion $m^3$ and the middle route 13 billion $m^3$. The east and middle routes have been respectively commenced in 2002 and 2003. Meanwhile, more efforts have been given to rural water supply and water safety. Up to the end of 2008, China has accumulatively provided drinking water to 272 million rural people, and clean drinking water to 165 million rural people, which primarily put an end to the drinking water scarcity history in rural areas. More than half of the rural population is now provided with tap water. The nationwide water supply capacity has jumped from 100 billion plus $m^3$ at the beginning of new China to 749.1 billion $m^3$, which makes a tremendous contribution to the national economic prosperity and social development.

塔里木河生态调水
Ecological Water Diversion in Tarim River

图 例 LEGEND

| | | | |
|---|---|---|---|
| 黑龙江流域 Heilong River Basin | | 长江流域 Yangtze River Basin | |
| 辽河流域 Liaohe River Basin | | 东南沿海诸河流域 Southeast River Basin | |
| 滦河流域 Luanhe River Basin | | 珠江流域 Pearl River Basin | |
| 海河流域 Haihe River Basin | | 沅江－红河流域 Yuanjiang River–Honghe River Basin | |
| 黄河流域 Yellow River Basin | | 澜沧江－湄公河流域 Lancang River–Mekong River Basin | |
| 淮河流域 Huaihe River Basin | | 怒江流域 Nujiang River Basin | |

我国调水工程示意图
Sketch Map of Water Transfer Projects in China

① 东深供水工程金湖泵站
Jinhu Pumping Station of Dongshen Water Supply Project

② 潘家口水库——引滦入津的水源工程
Panjiakou Reservoir, water source project of water transfer from the Luanhe River to Tianjin City

③ 引黄济青工程
Water Transfer Project from the Yellow River to Qingdao City

Chapter II Construction and Achievements 第二篇 建设与成就

85

Chapter II Construction and Achievements　第二篇　建设与成就

青海西宁第七供水厂

① 辽宁大连市沙河口水厂
Shahekou Water Supply Plant in Dalian City, Liaoning Province

② 促进城乡供水一体化的浙江诸暨市城南水厂
Chengnan Water Treatment Plant of Zhuji City, Zhejiang Province, which plays an important role in promoting integrated water supply to urban and rural areas

③ 青海西宁第七供水厂
7th Water Supply Plant, Xining City, Qinghai Province

Chapter II  Construction and Achievements  第二篇  建设与成就

① 南水北调工程东线、中线示意图
Sketch Map of the East and Middle Route of South-to-North Water Transfer Project

② 南水北调中线一期工程漕河渡槽出口通水
Water running through the outlet of aqueduct across Caohe River from the 1st stage of the Middle Route of South-to-North Water Transfer Project

③ 建成后的济平干渠
Completed Jiping Main Canal

④ 正在加紧建设的南水北调工程
South-to-North Water Transfer Project under construction

① 陕西农村供水工程
A rural water supply project in Shaanxi Province

② 重庆梁平县农村饮水安全工程
A rural safe drinking water project in Liangping County, Chongqing City

③ 河南新郑市农村饮水安全工程
A rural safe drinking water project in Xinzheng City, Henan Province

④ 四川通江县农村供水工程施工
Construction of a rural water supply project in Tongjiang County, Sichuan Province

⑤ 辽宁辽中县防氟改水工程设备
Equipment of fluorine resistant and water treatment project in Liaozhong County, Liaoning Province

⑥ 广西合浦县农村饮水安全工程
A rural safe drinking water project in Hepu County, Guangxi Zhuang Autonomous Region

Chapter II Construction and Achievements　第二篇　建设与成就

91

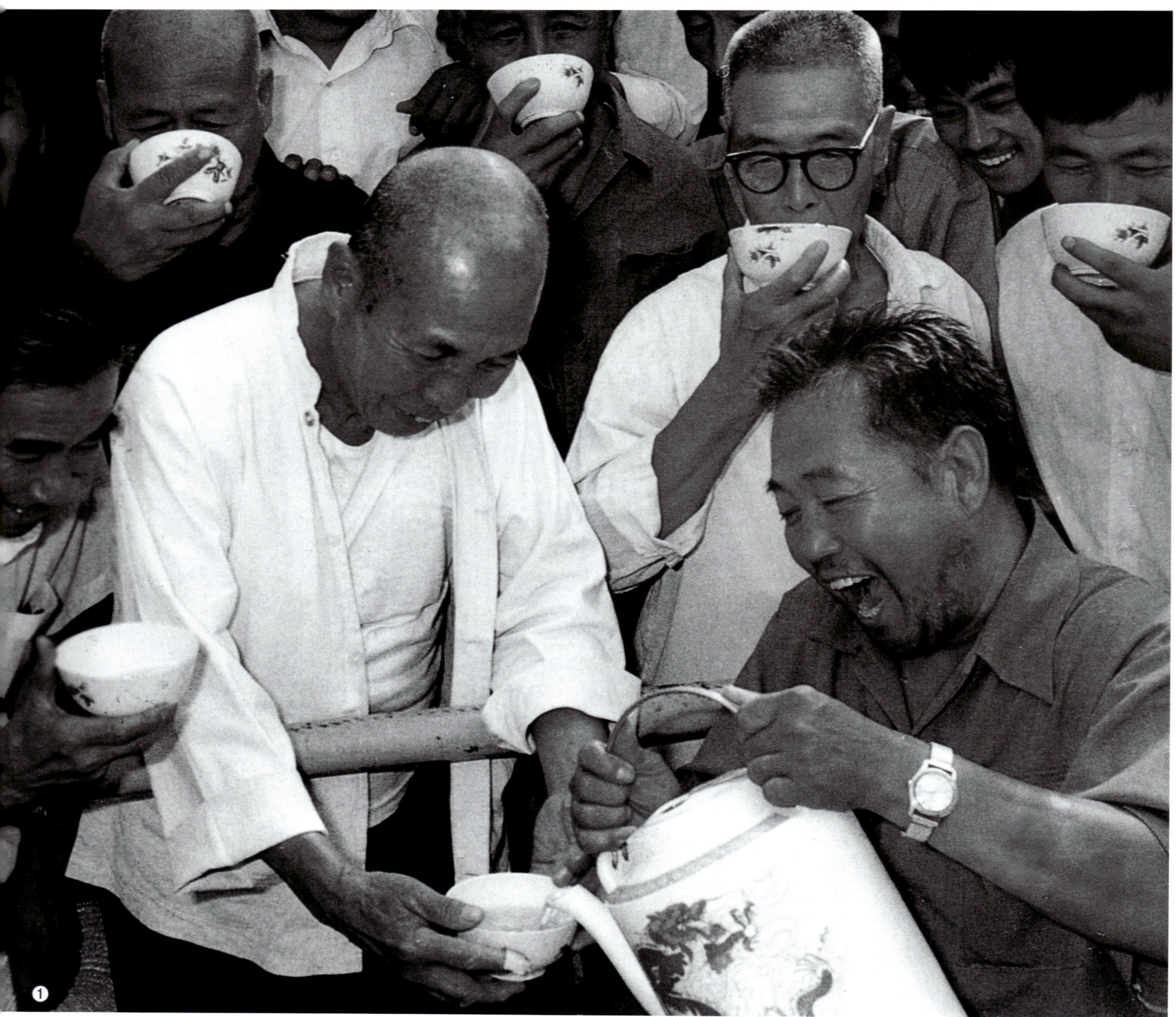

① 引滦入津工程结束了天津人民喝苦咸水的历史
The water transfer project from Luanhe River to Tianjin City ends the history of drinking brackish water in Tianjin City

② 东深供水保障了香港的繁荣稳定
Dongshen Water Supply Project guarantees the prosperity and stability of Hong Kong SAR

① 自来水进农家（河北）
Tap water running into the home of farmers (Hebei Province)

② 用上自来水让王老汉一家笑得合不上嘴（河南）
Mr Wang's family is very happy since they have gained access to tap water (Henan Province)

③ 西藏牧民喝上自来水
Provision of drinking water in pastureland in Tibet

③

2005年11月13日，中石油吉林石化分公司双苯厂苯胺装置发生爆炸事故，泄漏的化工原料随同消防废水流入第二松花江，造成松花江水污染。事件发生后，水利部门迅速采取措施，加强对松花江水体的实时动态监测，及时跟踪水体污染及行进情况；同时加大上游水库下泄流量，加快污染水团下行速度，稀释受污染水体。通过积极努力，有效应对了水污染造成的供水危机。

On November 13, 2005, the phenol installation in Jilin Petrochemical Company under Petro China blasted. The leaked chemical material and waste water from fire extinguishing flowed into and polluted the Songhua River. After the accident, the MWR made a quick response, enhanced the real time dynamic monitoring of the water body, increased the discharge flow of reservoirs in the upper reaches to increase discharging speed of the polluted water and diluted the pollutant, thus crisis of water supply was effectively resolved.

2007年5月29日，太湖流域贡湖水厂取水口因蓝藻暴发，引发无锡市供水危机。为保证流域供水安全，水利部门果断决策，加大太湖水质监测频度，实施引江济太水量调度，运用常熟水利枢纽等设施，尽最大可能调引长江好水入太湖，大大促进了水体交换，提高了太湖的环境容量，抑制了蓝藻生长，太湖北部水质明显好转，缓解了蓝藻暴发引发的供水危机。

On May 29, 2007, green algae exploded at the water intake of Gonghu Water Supply Plant in Taihu Lake severely threatened the water supply to Wuxi City. In order to ensure drinking water safety, the MWR made a quick and effective decision, i.e. to enhance water quality monitoring, divert water from the Yangtze River to Taihu Lake with the operation of Changshu Water Project to facilitate the exchange of water and improve the environmental capacity of Taihu Lake. Thanks to these measures, green algae were brought under control and water quality in north part of the Taihu Lake was obviously improved, and water supply pressure of the basin reduced.

近几年，每逢冬春季节，珠江河口咸潮上溯，导致珠江三角洲地区的澳门、珠海、中山等地区和城市出现供水危机。为此，水利部门联合调度珠江上游8座水库，实施了大规模的珠江压咸补淡应急调水措施。从2004年底至2009年初，先后5次组织了珠江流域压咸补淡应急调水，确保了澳门特区及广州、珠海、中山的供水安全。

In recent years, as a result of low flow, saltwater would intrude the estuary of the Pearl River in springs and winters, causing water supply crisis in delta region including Macau, Zhuhai and Zhongshan Cities. To resolve the issue, MWR made joint operation of 8 reservoirs in the upper reaches of the Pearl River to supplement fresh water for repelling saltwater. From the end of 2004 to the beginning of 2009, 5 emergency water transfers have been conducted so as to ensure water supply in the relevant cities and areas.

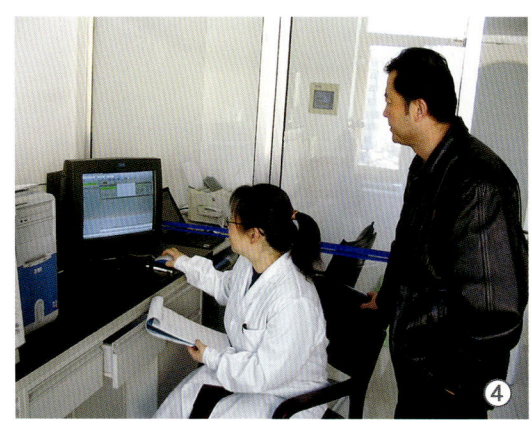

① 松辽流域水资源保护局成立了水污染事件应急处理调度室
Emergency control center set up by Songliao Water Resources Protection Bureau to look after Songhua River pollution accident

② 水利专家赴吉化公司爆炸现场排污口进行检查
Field inspection at sewage outlet by water experts after the Songhua River pollution accident

③ 监测人员进行断面水样采集
Sample collection by monitors at the river section

④ 应急跟踪监测临时实验室加强水质跟踪监测
Temporary Laboratory of emergency tracking and monitoring strengthens the water quality tracking and monitoring

① 太湖蓝藻
Green algae in Taihu Lake

② 水体蓝藻调查
Investigating green algae of water

③ 实验室水质分析试验
Water Quality Experimentation in the Lab

④ 常熟水利枢纽
Changshu Water Project

① 岩滩水库向下游调水
Yantan Reservoir diverting water to the lower reaches

② 珠江压咸补淡应急调水工程输水管
Pipelines of the Pearl River emergency water transfer project for repelling saltwater and supplementing freshwater

③ 水文监测在调水中发挥了重要作用
Hydrological monitoring plays an important role in water diversion

④ 澳门代表向水利部珠江水利委员会赠送牌匾
The representative of Macau presenting a tablet to Pearl River Water Resources Commission, MWR

## ◆ 农田水利建设
## Farmland Infrastructure Construction

新中国成立60年来，党和政府始终重视和加强农田水利建设，为促进农业发展和保证粮食安全提供了重要保障。新中国成立初期，以兴建水库拦蓄地表水源、提高河道防洪能力、发展农田灌溉为主，建成了一大批水利工程，为新中国经济社会的发展打下了基础。20世纪70年代，北方打井开发利用地下水，发展井灌，基本扭转了南粮北运的局面。南方地区依靠机电排灌技术，扩大灌溉面积，增加除涝面积。20世纪90年代以来，又以大力推广节水灌溉为重点，对大中型灌区进行续建配套和节水改造，对中低产田进行农业综合开发改造，对小型农村水利工程实施产权制度改革。

目前，我国已经建成设计灌溉面积超过30万亩的大型灌区447个，1万～30万亩的中型灌区5967个，小型农田水利工程2000多万处。全国农田有效灌溉面积从新中国成立时的2.4亿亩扩大到8.77亿亩，占世界总量的1/5，居世界首位。占全国耕地48%的灌溉面积，生产了占全国总产量75%的粮食和90%的棉花、蔬菜等经济作物，灌区成为我国粮食安全保障的重要基地。

Over the past 60 years, the Chinese government has always attached great importance to farmland infrastructure construction to ensure agricultural development and food security. Since 1949, a large number of infrastructures, including reservoirs for surface water storage, projects for flood defense and irrigation were built, which laid a solid foundation for socio-economic development. In the 1970s, through digging wells for groundwater utilization in the north, Northern China was able to rely on itself for grain supply. Southern China developed electro-mechanical irrigation technologies, expanded irrigated area and increased waterlogging area. Since the 1990s, China further promoted water-saving irrigation, conducted counterpart projects and water-saving projects construction in large and medium sized irrigation districts, developed and upgraded low-yield farmland and implemented ownership reform of small water projects.

At present, China has 447 large-scale irrigation districts exceeding 0.3 million *mu*, 5,967 medium-sized irrigated areas from 0.1 million to 0.3 million *mu*, and over 20 million small-scale water projects. Irrigated area has increased from 240 million *mu* in 1949 to 877 million *mu* at present, accounting 1/5 of the world total and ranking 1st among all countries. Irrigated area takes up 48% of total farmland in China, producing 75% of grain and 90% of economic crop in the country. Irrigation districts have become important bases for China's food security.

我国大型灌区分布图
Map of Large-scale Irrigation Districts Layout

① 四川都江堰灌区——我国特大型灌区之一，实际灌溉面积1134万亩
Dujiangyan Irrigation District is one of the mega irrigation districts in China, with a total irrigated area of 11.34 million *mu*

② 江苏江都排灌站——我国最大的排灌泵站，总装机容量49800千瓦
Jiangdu Irrigation and Drainage Station in Jiangsu Province is the biggest electric irrigation and drainage pumping station with a total installed capacity of 49,800 kW

兴利除害 富国惠民 ——新中国水利60年
Generate Benefits and Mitigate Hazards to Contribute to the Prosperity of the Nation and the Interests of the People
——60 Years' Water Development in China

① 河南人民胜利渠——新中国成立后在黄河下游兴建的第一个大型引黄灌溉工程。图为人民胜利渠渠首
Renmin Shengli Canal, the first large-scale irrigation project diverting Yellow River water for irrigation in the lower reaches of the Yellow River after 1949

② 安徽淠史杭灌区——我国特大型灌区之一，实际灌溉面积1000万亩
Pishihang Irrigation District, locating in Anhui Province, is one of the mega irrigation districts in China, with an irrigated area of 10 million *mu*

③ 宁夏青铜峡引黄灌区——开创于秦汉时期，是我国最古老的引黄灌区，实际灌溉面积506万亩，1967年建成的青铜峡水利枢纽，结束了灌区无坝引水的历史
Qingtongxia Irrigation District in Ningxia Hui Autonomous Region, was constructed in Qin and Han Dynasties. It was the eldest Qingtongxia Water Project using Yellow River water for irrigation. The irrigated area is 5.06 million *mu*. The Qingtongxia Water Project built in 1967 was the first dam to divert water to the area

Chapter II  Construction and Achievements  第二篇　建设与成就

① 内蒙古河套灌区——我国特大型灌区之一，实际灌溉面积860万亩
  Hetao Irrigation District in Inner Mongolia Autonomous Region, one of mega irrigation districts with a total irrigated area of 8.6 million *mu*

② 山东邹平引黄干渠节水改造
  Water-saving and upgrading project of water diversion channel from the Yellow River in Zouping City, Shandong Province

③ 实施节水改造后的宁夏灌区第一大渠——唐徕渠
  Tanglai Canal, after water-saving and upgrading, is the largest canal in Ningxia Irrigation District

① 内蒙古西辽河灌区
West Liaohe Irrigation District in Inner Mongolia Autonomous Region

② 黑龙江引汤灌区渠首
Headworks of Yintang Irrigation District in Heilongjiang Province

③ 江苏扬州市百万亩节水农田
Water-saving farmland, Yangzhou City, Jiangsu Province

① 广西蔬菜喷灌
Spray irrigation in Guangxi Zhuang Autonomous Region

② 贵州小型农田水利工程
Some small water projects in Guizhou Province

③ 湖南韶山灌区输水渡槽
An aqueduct in Shaoshan Irrigation District, Hunan Province

④ 新疆生产建设兵团大型喷灌机
Large-scale Sprinkling Irrigation Machine by Xinjiang Production and Construction Corps

⑤ 甘肃张掖市灌区农民用水者协会
A Farmer Association of Water Use of Zhangye City, Gansu Province

① 美丽富饶的江汉平原
　　Beautiful and affluent Jianghan Plain
② 灌区农业丰收的景象
　　Harvesting scene in an irrigation district

## ◆ 水土流失治理
## Water and Soil Loss Control

我国是世界上水土流失最严重的国家之一，全国现有水土流失面积356万平方千米，占国土总面积的37.1%，每年流失土壤45亿多吨，损失耕地100多万亩。新中国成立以来，党和政府领导人民开展了大规模的水土流失综合治理，取得了举世瞩目的成就。60年来，全国累计初步治理水土流失面积101.6万平方千米，实施治理小流域5万多条，建成黄土高原淤地坝9万多座，国家水土保持重点工程覆盖了600多个水土流失严重县。全国实施水土保持生态修复72万平方千米，加快了水土流失治理步伐。现有水土保持措施每年可保持土壤15亿吨，增加蓄水能力250多亿立方米，增产粮食180亿千克，惠及1亿多人，促使5000多万群众摆脱贫困。凡是经过水土流失重点治理的地区，都取得了明显的生态、经济和社会效益，给群众带来了实实在在的利益。

China is one of the countries suffering most severe water and soil erosion problems with a total of 3.56 million km² erosion areas occupying 37.1% of the total territory. Every year more than 4.5 billion tons of soil were lost and more than 1 million *mu* of arable land reduced. During the past 60 years since the founding of new China, the Chinese government has mobilized large-scale comprehensive rehabilitation and made world known achievements. 1.016 million km² and more than 50,000 small watersheds restored, more than 90,000 check dams constructed and the nation's key water and soil conservation projects covering more than 600 key counties suffering severe water and soil loss. An area of 720,000 km² has been ecologically restored which help speed up the pace of erosion control. The current water and soil conservation measures can annually retain 1.5 billion tons of soil and increase water storage capacity by more than 25 billion m³ and grain production by 18 billion kg benefiting more than 100 million people and help a population of more than 50 million get rid of poverty. All those people in key rehabilitated areas have witnessed obvious ecological, economic and social benefits.

江西安远县小流域综合治理
Comprehensive rehabilitation of small watersheds in Anyuan County, Jiangxi Province

Chapter II  Construction and Achievements 第二篇 建设与成就

1991年《中华人民共和国水土保持法》颁布实施，水土保持工作逐步走上依法防治轨道。60年来，全国累计开展水土保持执法检查5.2万次，查处违法案件1万多起，共审批生产建设项目水土保持方案25万多项，全国1.5万千米新建公路、1.2万千米新建铁路实施了水土保持方案。社会各界的水土保持法制观念明显加强，人为水土流失在一定程度上得到遏制。

水土保持监测工作从无到有，逐步推开。先后开展了三次全国水土流失遥感普查，基本摸清了全国水土流失情况和动态趋势。初步建成了由水利部水土保持监测中心、7个流域中心站、29个省级总站和151个分站组成的水土保持监测网络。水土流失监测预报能力显著增强，从2003年起连续7年发布全国及部分省区水土保持公报，为社会提供服务和参考。

① 长江上中游水土保持重点防治工程——湖北丹江口市水土保持示范项目区
A pilot area of key project of water and soil conservation in the upper and middle reaches of the Yangtze River Basin in Danjiangkou City, Hubei Province

② 甘肃庄浪县梯田
Terrace in Zhuanglang County, Gansu Province

Water and Soil Conservation Law was promulgated in 1991, providing legal guidance to water and soil conservation work. In the past 60 years, 52,000 times law enforcement inspection have been conducted and more than 10,000 law violation cases have been punished. Meanwhile, more than 250,000 items of water and soil conservation plan have been approved. It has been required to practice soil conservation in the 12,000 km newly built railways and 15,000 km of newly built highways. With more legal awareness of water and soil conservation, man-made water and soil erosion has been prevented to some extent.

Monitoring on water and soil conservation is gradually becoming a routine practice. Three nationwide general investigations by remote sensing primarily clarified the situation and dynamic situation in the country. The monitoring network consisting of Water and Soil Conservation Monitoring Center of MWR, 7 river basin level stations, 29 provincial stations and 151 branches has been fundamentally established, with which water and soil conservation monitoring and forecast capability has improved dramatically. Since 2003, 7 communiqués on water and soil conservation for the whole nation and some provinces have been publicized, which provided a reference to the society.

① 

②

③

Chapter II Construction and Achievements 第二篇 建设与成就

① 贵州盘县木车小流域治理
Rehabilitation of Muche small watershed in Panxian County, Guizhou Province

② 长江流域坡改梯促进粮食增收
Turning slope into terrace to increase the grain productivity in the Yangtze River Basin

③ 宁夏彭阳县小河小流域综合治理
Comprehensive rehabilitation of small watersheds in Pengyang County, Ningxia Hui Autonomous Region

① 治理世界风库——甘肃瓜州
Rehabilitation of Guazhou County, Gansu Province, a world famous windy area

② 沙棘治理砒砂岩水土流失促进群众增收。图为群众采摘沙棘果
Seabuckthorn grown on sandstone increases people's income while controlling erosion. The picture shows the scene of harvesting seabuckthorn

③ 黑龙江拜泉县小流域治理黑土地水土流失
Water and soil conservation on black soil in small watersheds in Baiquan County, Heilongjiang Province

④ 重庆云阳县水土流失治理成果
Achievement of water and soil conservation in Yunyang County, Chongqing City

④

① 北京生态清洁型小流域
  Clean Ecological Small Watershed in Beijing City
② 黑龙江宾县水土保持径流观测场
  Water and soil conservation runoff observation field in Binxian County, Heilongjiang Province
③ 广西百色市高速公路水土保持工程
  Highway water and soil conservation project in Baise City, Guangxi Zhuang Autonomous Region

①② 山西偏关县水土保持项目区治理前后
Before and after water and soil conservation in project area in Pianguan County, Shanxi Province

③④ 辽宁朝阳市乌兰河硕小流域治理前后
Before and after rehabilitation of Wulanheshuo small watershed in Chaoyang City, Liaoning Province

⑤ 陕西淤地坝拦沙淤地
Check dams in Shaanxi Province

⑥ 贵州水土保持项目区发展茶园
Tea garden in water and soil conservation project area in Guizhou Province

Chapter II Construction and Achievements 第二篇 建设与成就

123

## 生态文明建设
## Construction of Ecological Civilization

水资源是基础性的自然资源和战略性的经济资源，也是生态环境的控制性要素。在可持续发展治水思路指导下，水利部门坚持人与自然和谐，把促进生态文明建设放在水利工作更加突出的位置，开展了以水利措施修复生态与环境的实践。通过依法统一调度和科学配置水资源，实现了黄河连续10年不断流，黑河下游东居延海连续5年不干涸，塔里木河下游生态逐年恢复；向南四湖、扎龙、向海、白洋淀等湖泊或湿地实施应急补水，保护和修复了生态系统；开展了引江济太、淮河闸坝防污调度，改善水体水质，减少水污染损失。大力开展城乡水环境整治，利用水利工程的多功能性，改善城乡水生态，打造亲水人居环境，加强水利风景区建设，努力满足广大人民群众实现优质生活、享有优良环境的需求。

Water resources are the fundamental natural resources and strategic economic resources as well as controlling element of eco-environment. Under the guidance of the concept of sustainable water resources management, water resources management departments adhere to the harmonization between human and nature, pay more attention to the construction of ecological civilization and undertake the practice of restoring the ecology and environment with water conservancy measures. Thanks to integrated dispatch and scientific allocation of water resources, Yellow River never experienced zero flow in the past 10 consecutive years, the East Juyan Lake in the lower reaches of the Heihe River never dried up in the past 5 consecutive years, the ecology in the lower reaches of the Tarim River gradually restored, and the eco-system in Nansihu Lake, Zhalong Wetlands, Xianghai Wetlands and Baiyangdian Lake have been well protected and restored through emergent water diversion. Meanwhile, by means of water transfer from the Yangtze River to the Taihu Lake and water diversion through the Huaihe River water locks, water quality was improved and water pollution was mitigated. By rehabilitating the rural and urban water environment, taking advantage of the multi-functions of water works, the rural and urban water eco-systems have been improved. Unremitting efforts are being made to build comfortable living environment along riverbanks so as to meet the demand of the people and environment.

① 实施调水后东居延海周边芦苇面积不断扩大
The area of reeds along East Juyan Lake extends after the implementation of water transfer

② 水资源统一调度使塔里木河下游生态逐渐恢复
Integrated water resources dispatch help to improve ecology in the lower reaches of the Tarim River

Chapter II  Construction and Achievements  第二篇  建设与成就

① 黄河河口实施补水后生态得以恢复
  Ecology of the Yellow River Estuary restored after water supplement
② 应急补水后的白洋淀生态恢复
  Ecology of Baiyangdian Lake restored after emergent water supplement
③ 对扎龙湿地实施补水
  Water is flowing into the Zhalong Wetlands
④ 扎龙湿地补水后生机盎然
  Zhalong Wetlands is full of life

① 北京水景观
　Water landscape in Beijing City

② 天津海河夜景
　Night view of Haihe River in Tianjin City

③ 整治后的上海苏州河
　Suzhou River in Shanghai City after rehabilitation

①

②

① 治理后的广东深圳河
  Shenzhen River after rehabilitation in Guangdong Province
② 整治后的江苏泰兴市村乡河塘
  A rural pond after rehabilitation in Taixing City, Jiangsu Province

兴利除害 富国惠民 ——新中国水利60年
Generate Benefits and Mitigate Hazards to Contribute to the Prosperity of the Nation and the Interests of the People
—— 60 Years' Water Development in China

① 整治后的浙江嘉善县村乡河塘
A rural pond after rehabilitation in Jiashan County, Zhejiang Province

② 国家水利风景区——江西井冈山井冈湖
Jinggang Lake in Jinggangshan City of Jiangxi Province, a National Level Water Park

## 水能资源开发
### Development of Hydro Resources

我国水能资源蕴藏量居世界首位。新中国成立时，除东北伪满时期修建的丰满、水丰、镜泊湖水电站外，我国几乎没有大水电，1949年底全国水电装机总量仅列世界第20位。新中国成立后，党和政府高度重视水能资源的开发利用，尤其是改革开放以来，我国坚持节约资源、保护环境的基本国策，在合理规划的基础上结合江河治理兴建了一大批水电站。截至2008年底，我国已建水电装机容量达到1.72亿千瓦，位居世界第一，年发电量5633亿千瓦时，占全国总发电装机的22%、总发电量的16%左右，水电设计、施工和设备制造技术均已达到国际先进水平。水电的发展在增加我国能源供应、改善能源结构、保护生态环境、减少温室气体排放方面做出了重要贡献。

China's hydropower potential ranks at the first place in the world. When new China was founded, there were hardly any large hydropower stations existed except Fengman, Shuifeng, Jingpohu hydropower stations constructed in the northeast China in the Manchuria Period. At the end of 1949, the total installed hydropower capacity only ranked at the 20th in the world. Since the founding of new China, especially after the reform and opening up policy, the Chinese government have attached great importance to the development of hydropower and constructed a great number of hydropower stations on the basis of scientific planning in compliance with the national policy of energy saving and environment protection. By the end of 2008, the installed capacity of the completed hydropower stations reached 172 million kW, ranking the first in the world, with the annual hydropower generation of 563.3 billion kW·h, 22% of the nation's total installed capacity and around 16% of the total power generation. The capacities of design, construction and equipment manufacturing are all among the top in the world. The development of hydropower has made an important contribution to the energy supply, energy structure improvement, environment protection and reduction of greenhouse gas emission.

黄河龙羊峡水电站——黄河上游第一座大型梯级电站，水库总容量247亿立方米，总装机容量128万千瓦，位于青海省

Longyangxia Hydropower Station, the first large cascade project on the upper reaches of the Yellow River, with a total reservoir storage capacity of 24.7 billion m³ and total installed power generation capacity of 1.28 million kW, is located in Qinghai Province

① 新安江水电站——新中国成立后建设的第一座大型水电站，水库总库容220亿立方米，总装机容量66.25万千瓦，位于浙江省
Xin'anjiang Hydropower Station, the first large hydropower station after the establishment of New China, with total storage capacity of 22 billion m³ and installed capacity of 662.5 MW, is located in Zhejiang Province

② 龙滩水电站——国内在建的仅次于三峡的特大型水电工程，水库总库容273亿立方米，总装机容量630万千瓦，位于广西壮族自治区
Longtan Hydropower Station, the 2nd largest one under construction ranked after the Three Gorges Project, with a total storage capacity of 27.3 billion m³ and an installed capacity of 6.3 million kW, is located in Guangxi Zhuang Autonomous Region

③ 二滩水电站——水库总库容58亿立方米，总装机容量330万千瓦。其双曲拱坝坝高在同类坝型中居亚洲第一、世界第三，位于四川省
Ertan Hydropower Station, with a total storage capacity of 5.8 billion m³ and total installed capacity of 3.3 million kW. Its dam height lists the first in Asia and 3rd in the world compared with all the other double curvature arch dams, and it is located in Sichuan Province

我国农村水能资源十分丰富，改革开放以来，党和政府十分重视发展农村水电，加快农村水电及电气化县建设。进入21世纪，为巩固退耕还林等生态建设成果，解决农民燃料和长远致富问题，国家又实施了小水电代燃料工程，探索了一条农村水能资源开发与生态建设有效结合的新路子，试点山区20多万户、80多万农民彻底告别了祖祖辈辈上山砍柴、烟熏火燎的日子，同时保护森林面积350多万亩，被群众誉为点亮大山希望的德政工程。截至2008年底，我国已建成农村水电站45000座，装机容量达5100多万千瓦，年发电量1600多亿千瓦时，约占我国水电装机和年发电量的30%、世界小水电总装机容量的一半以上，通过开发农村水能资源，累计解决了3亿多无电人口的用电问题，农村水电地区的户通电率从1980年的不足40%提高到2008年的99.6%，农村水电遍布全国1/2的地域、1/3的县市。

① 吉林双山水电站
   Shuangshan Hydropower Station in Jilin Province
② 湖南茶陵县青年水电站
   Youth Hydropower Station in Chaling County of Hunan Province
③ 河南崛山水电站
   Jueshan Hydropower Station in Henan Province
④ 安徽皖南山区小水电站
   A small hydropower plant in southern mountainous area of Anhui Province
⑤ 浙江景宁县高水头水电站——景润水电站
   Jingrun Hydropower Station, with high head Jingning County of Zhejiang Province

There are rich hydro potential in rural China. After the adoption of the policy of reform and opening up, Chinese government attached importance to the development of rurual hydropower, and speeded up the steps of electrification county. After entering the 21st century, in order to consolidate the achievements of returning the cultivated land to forestry and to solve farmers' fuel problems and upgrade their living standard, China began to conduct the Replacing Firewood with Small Hydropower Project, which help to pave way for combined benefits of rural hydropower development together with the ecosystem improvement. The pilot project brings benefit to 200 thousand households and 800 thousand farmers enabling them quit the life for ever when they had to chop woods for fuel. Moreover 3.5 million *mu* of forestry were protected. Therefore, the project, lighting the remote mountains, was highly appreciated and welcomed by the people. Up to the end of 2008, China has constructed 45,000 rural hydropower stations, with total installed capacity of 51 million kW and annual power generation 160 billion kW·h, which accounts to 30% of the national figure both in terms of installed capacity and power generation and 1/2 of the total world small hydropower installation. Along with rural hydropower development, 300 million of population obtained the access to electricity. The percentage of households to electricity was increased from 40% in 1980 to 99.6% in 2008. The rural hydropower has covered half of China and 1/3 of the counties.

Chapter II Construction and Achievements 第二篇 建设与成就

① 实施小水电代燃料项目前，农民做饭烟熏火燎
Before the Replacing Firewood with Small Hydropower Project, farmers cooked with firewood

② 实施小水电代燃料项目后，农户厨房焕然一新
After the Project, farmers' kitchen takes up a new look

③ 广东连山县电气化县建设成果
Electrification brings a flourishing life in Lianshan County, Guangdong Province

④ 农村水电及电气化县建设使农村居民精神面貌发生巨大变化
The rural hydropower development and electrification at the county level changed a lot the life of the local people a lot

# 第三篇　防灾与减灾

我国是世界上自然灾害最为严重的国家之一，水旱灾害更是中华民族长期以来的心腹之患。特殊的地理气候条件使得我国洪涝、干旱、台风、山洪、泥石流等灾害频繁发生，水旱灾害造成的损失和影响位居我国各类自然灾害之首。

新中国成立以来，党和政府领导人民与水旱灾害进行了不懈斗争，取得了举世瞩目的成就。特别是近年来，党中央、国务院把防汛抗旱减灾当作改善民生的大事和要事来抓，不断总结治水经验，创新工作机制，防汛抗旱减灾并举，工程措施非工程措施并重，推动防汛抗旱工作由控制洪水向洪水管理转变，由单一抗旱向全面抗旱转变，水旱灾害综合防御能力明显提高。在体制机制方面，初步形成了统一指挥、反应灵敏、协调有序、运转高效的应急管理机制；在工程体系方面，全国大江大河主要河段已基本具备了防御新中国成立以来最大洪水的能力，重点海堤按50年一遇标准建设，遇到中等干旱年份，工农业生产和生态用水不会受到大的影响，可以基本保证城乡供水安全；在预报预警方面，建立了较为完善的大江大河主要河段洪水预报系统，初步建立了全国旱情监测系统；在预案建设方面，建立了国家防汛抗旱预案体系，有防汛抗旱任务的县级以上政府都制定了防汛抗旱应急预案；在法律法规方面，形成了以水法、防洪法和抗旱条例为核心的防汛抗旱法律法规体系；在队伍保障方面，初步形成专群结合、军民结合的防汛抗旱抢险队伍。依靠逐步完善的防汛抗旱减灾综合体系和全社会的广泛参与，成功战胜了历次特大洪水和严重干旱，有效应对了频繁发生的台风和山洪灾害袭击，有效保障了防洪安全、供水安全和粮食安全，最大程度地减轻了灾害损失，保障了经济社会全面协调可持续发展。

# Chapter III
# Disaster Prevention and Mitigation

China is one of the countries experiencing the most severe natural disasters. The flood and drought are the serious hidden trouble of China. The special geographic and climate conditions result in the frequent disasters such as flood, drought, typhoon, flash flood, and mud flow. The loss and impact of flood and drought rank first compared with other natural disasters.

After the founding of new China in 1949, the Chinese government and people fought against the flood and drought with remarkable achievements. Especially in recent years, the central government has taken the flood control and drought relief as the most important issue for the people's livelihood improvement. On the basis of experiences summary, the government has reformed the working mechanism, adopted both the engineering and non-engineering measures, and facilitated the change from flood control to flood management and for the unitary drought relief measures to the comprehensive one so as to highly improve the integrated flood and drought disaster prevention and control. In the aspect of mechanism, the emergency management mechanism featuring the unified command, fast reaction, effective coordination and efficient functioning has been preliminarily shaped. In terms of engineering system, the major reaches of large rivers have the capacity to fight against the biggest flood since the founding of new China. The major sea dikes have been constructed according to the standard of fighting against the disasters with a return period of 50 years. So that in the years with moderate drought of the industrial and agricultural production, as well as the ecosystem, will not be seriously affected and the urban and rural water supply guaranteed. The flood forecasting and warning system for the major reaches of large rivers and the national drought monitoring system have been established. The working plan, the national flood control and drought relief plans have been completed, and the same for the counties and the above as well. In terms of legislation, the laws and regulations for enacted flood control and drought relief with the Water Law, Flood Control Law and Drought Relief as the key have been enacted. And in the field of human resources, an emergency team combining the professionals, the public, the army and the civilians has been formed. Relying on the improved comprehensive flood control and drought relief system and the extensive public participation, we conquered each large flood and severe drought, effectively fought against the frequent typhoons and flash floods, guaranteed the security of flood control, water supply and food production, mitigated the disaster losses, and ensured the sustainable economic and social development in a comprehensive way.

# 我国防汛抗旱组织机构示意图
## Sketch map of flood control and drought relief organization

- **国家防汛抗旱总指挥部** — The State Flood Control and Drought Relief Headquarters
  - **流域防汛抗旱指挥机构** — The flood control and drought relief headquarters at river basin level
    - 长江防汛抗旱总指挥部 — The Yangtze River Flood Control and Drought Relief Headquarters
    - 黄河防汛抗旱总指挥部 — The Yellow River Flood Control and Drought Relief Headquarters
    - 淮河防汛总指挥部 — The Huaihe River Flood Control Headquarters
    - 海河防汛抗旱总指挥部 — The Haihe River Flood Control and Drought Relief Headquarters
    - 珠江防汛抗旱总指挥部 — The Pearl River Flood Control and Drought Relief Headquarters
    - 松花江防汛抗旱总指挥部 — The Songhua River Flood Control and Drought Relief Headquarters
    - 太湖流域防汛抗旱总指挥部 — The Taihu Lake Basin Flood Control and Drought Relief Headquarters
  - **省级防汛抗旱指挥机构** — The flood control and drought relief headquarters at provincial level
    - **地市级防汛抗旱指挥机构** — The flood control and drought relief command agencies at municipal level
      - **县级防汛抗旱指挥机构** — The flood control and drought relief command agencies at county level
        - **乡村防汛抗旱组织** — The rural flood control and drought relief organizations

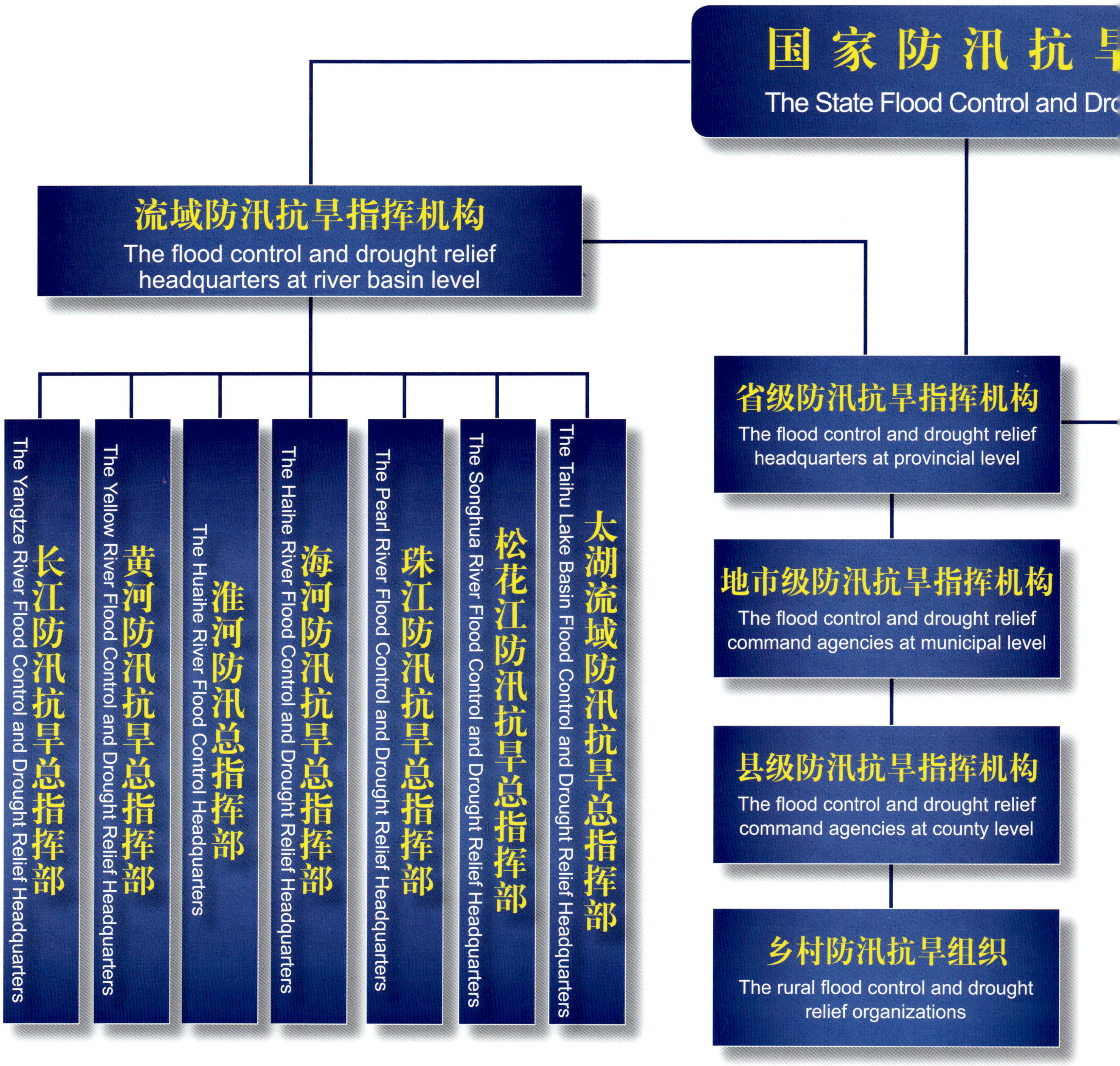

# 组织机构示意图
## ...d drought relief organizations

**总指挥部** / ...nt Relief Headquarters

- 中共中央宣传部 / The Ministry of Publicity of CCCP
- 国家发展和改革委员会 / National Development and Reform Commission
- 工业和信息化部 / Ministry of Industry and Information Technology
- 公安部 / Ministry of Public Security
- 民政部 / Ministry of Civil Affairs
- 财政部 / Ministry of Finance
- 国土资源部 / Ministry of Land and Resources
- 住房和城乡建设部 / Ministry of Housing and Urban-Rural Development
- 交通运输部 / Ministry of Transport
- 铁道部 / Ministry of Railways
- 水利部 / Ministry of Water Resources
  - 长江水利委员会 / Changjiang Water Resources Commission
  - 黄河水利委员会 / Yellow River Conservancy Commission
  - 淮河水利委员会 / Huaihe River Conservancy Commission
  - 海河水利委员会 / Haihe Water Conservation Commission
  - 珠江水利委员会 / Pearl Water Conservation Commission
  - 松辽水利委员会 / Songliao Water Conservation Commission
  - 太湖流域管理局 / Taihu Lake Authority
- 农业部 / Ministry of Agriculture
- 商务部 / Ministry of Commerce
- 卫生部 / The Ministry of Health
- 国家广播电影电视总局 / State Administration of Radio, Film and Television
- 国家安全生产监督管理总局 / State Administration of Work Safety
- 中国气象局 / China Meteorological Administration
- 国家海洋局 / State Oceanic Administration
- 总参作战部 / Operations Department of the General Staff of PLA
- 武警部队 / Armed Police Force

- 省级政府有关部门及驻军 / Relevant departments and the garrison at provincial level
- 地市级政府有关部门及驻军 / Relevant departments and the garrison at municipal level
- 县级政府有关部门及驻军 / Relevant departments and the garrison at county level

### 洪涝灾害防控
### Prevention and Control of Floods and Water-logging

新中国成立以来，全国共修建加固堤防28.7万千米，建成水库8.64万座，主要蓄滞洪区97处，水文测站3.4万余处、报汛站点8600多个。已建成的各类水库和江河堤防可保护人口5.7亿人，保护耕地6.9亿亩。随着大江大河的治理、江河防洪标准的提高，江河决堤、洪水泛滥、肆虐成灾的局面得到根本扭转，主要江河中下游发展成为中国重要的工农业生产基地，防洪减灾效益显著。

据统计分析，1949年以来我国发生较大洪水50多次，按照2000年不变价格估算，全国七大江河以及太湖流域防洪减灾的直接经济效益达3.93万亿元，防洪减淹耕地面积24.75亿亩，平均每年减淹耕地4110万亩，年均减免粮食损失1029万吨，累计减免粮食损失6.17亿吨，每年因洪涝灾害死亡人数呈大幅度减少趋势。

Since the founding of the new China, Chinese government constructed and strengthened 287 thousand km of embankments, 86.4 thousand reservoirs, 97 major flood detention areas, 34 thousand hydrological stations and 8.6 thousand of flood forecasting stations. The existing reservoirs and dams could protect 570 million of population and 0.69 billion *mu* of cultivated lands. The management of major rivers and the improvement of flood control standards help prevent the dam failure. And the middle and lower reaches of major rivers become important industrial and agricultural centers with notable benefits from flood control and disaster relief.

According to the statistics, there have been 50 large floods since 1949. Accounting with the fixed price of 2000, the direct economic benefit from the flood control and drought relief of the 7 major rivers and the Taihu Lake reached 3.93 thousand billion *Yuan*, 2.475 billion *mu* of areas were prevented from submerging with an annual rate of 41.1 million *mu* hectares. And 617 million tons of food loss has been reduced with an annual rate of 10.29 million tons. The annual death toll caused by flood was markedly reduced as well.

① 洪水来袭
　The coming flood

② 水文职工抢测洪峰
　Hydrological staffs are monitoring peak flood

③ 水利职工24小时密切注视雨情、水情
　The 24-hour monitoring of rainfall and water regime

④⑤ 中央防汛物资仓库储备的抢险物资
　Emergency materials in the central flood control materials storehouse

## 1998：铸就伟大抗洪精神

1998年长江发生了继1954年以来的又一次全流域性大洪水。长江干流360千米江段和洞庭湖、鄱阳湖水位多次超过历史最高记录0.55～1.25米。嫩江干流全线和松花江干流的哈尔滨等站均超过历史最高洪水位，超出幅度最高达1.61米。长江上游接连出现8次洪峰，部分河段超过历史最高水位的时间长达40多天，嫩江、松花江干流超警戒水位长达两个多月。

在党中央、国务院的正确领导下，全国军民发扬"万众一心、众志成城、不怕困难、顽强拼搏、坚忍不拔、敢于胜利"的伟大抗洪精神，抗御了一次又一次洪水袭击，保护了人民群众的生命安全，保护了重要堤防、重要城市、主要交通干线的安全，取得了抗洪抢险斗争的全面胜利，创造了在特大洪水情况下将灾害损失减少到最低限度的历史奇迹。

## 1998: The Great Spirit of Fighting against Flood

In 1998, the whole Yangtze River basin was encountered with another large flood since 1954. The water levels of the Yangtze River's main stream of 360 km, Dongting Lake and Poyang Lake exceeded the historical highest records of 0.55-1.25 m for several times. The same situation also happened on the main stream of Nenjiang River and Harbin station of Songhua River, with the rising level peaked at 1.61 m. The upper reaches of the Yangtze River were faced with 8 flood peaks. The water level of some reaches exceeded the historical records with almost 40 days. And the water levels of Nenjiang River and Songhua River exceeded the warning line with more than 2 months.

Under the correct leadership of the central government, the army and the public realized the spirit of working together and being united as a wall, conquered the attacks of flood, protected the lives of the people, and ensured the safety of significant embankments, cities and major communication lines. The success in flood control created the historical miracle of reducing the loss to the minimum.

① 1998年8月7日，经过50多天洪水浸泡，长江大堤江西九江段溃决，滔滔江水汹涌泄出。危急时刻，人民子弟兵挺身而出，抢堵决口。图为九江决口抢堵誓师大会

On August 7, 1998, the Yangtze River embankment in Jiujiang reach failed after the water logging of 50 days. The flood poured out. The armymen blocked up the dike breaches. The picture shows the kick-off party for blocking up the dike breaches in Jiujiang

② 镇江铁牛望江兴叹

The ferric bull in Zhenjiang was submerged on the Yangtze River

③ 紧急调运抢险物资

The transportation of emergency materials

④ 众志成城

Unity is strength

⑤ 洪水中托起生命

Saving a life in the flood

九江长江大堤堵口现场
The scene of blocking up the breaches of Jiujiang Dike

① 经过5个昼夜顽强拼搏，九江长江大堤决口封堵成功

The breaches of Jiujiang Dike were blocked up successively after the 5 day-and-night combat

② 堤外洪水滚滚，堤内安然无恙 —— 1998年长江大水中的南京市

Flood was flowing out of the embankment, while the city was safe in the embankment—the Nanjing City in the large flood of 1998

③ 1931年大水时的武汉关

The Wuhan Barrier in the large flood of 1931

④ 1954年大水时的武汉关

The Wuhan Barrier in the large flood of 1954

⑤ 1998年大水时的武汉关

The Wuhan Barrier in the large flood of 1998

Chapter III Disaster Prevention and Mitigation 第三篇 防灾与减灾

153

## 2007：科学防控淮河大水

2007年淮河发生了新中国成立以来仅次于1954年的全流域性大洪水。2007年7月10日11时，素有淮河洪水"风向标"之称的王家坝，水位高达29.38米，超过国务院批准的分洪水位0.08米。此时，王家坝上游河南段淮河干支流堤防已出现险情150多处，洪汝河已全面超保证水位；下游正阳关、洪泽湖等水位也在快速上涨——汛情紧急！形势严峻！淮河抗洪面临着分洪还是继续严防死守的抉择。

在抗洪的紧要关头，国家防汛抗旱总指挥部根据雨情、水情和工情，科学研判，果断决策：开启王家坝闸分洪，启用蒙洼蓄洪区。科学、果断的决策，赢得了淮河抗洪的主动权。2007年7月11日，淮河干流洪峰顺利通过王家坝，洪水按照人们的意愿驯服下泄。此次淮河大水紧急转移80多万人，取得了行蓄洪区人民无一伤亡、淮河干流和重要支流堤防无一处决口、流域大小水库无一垮坝的骄人成绩。

2007年科学防控淮河大水，是以人为本、人水和谐、给洪水以出路的科学理念在防汛抗洪中的具体实践。今天的水利人不仅仅重视加固堤防、建设水库等工程，以约束、控制洪水，还主动退堤还河（湖）、兴建行蓄洪区、移民建镇，自觉给洪水安排出路，管理洪水。蒙洼的主动分洪，虽淹没了18万亩耕地，转移了区内3684名临时生产群众，换来的却是沿淮千万人的平安，保住的是沿淮城市、工矿企业和交通干线的安全。

① 国家防汛抗旱总指挥部科学研判、果断决策
The State Flood Control and Drought Relief Headquarters made the decision on the basis of the scientific studies

② 临淮岗移民新村。2003年大水后，淮河流域实施了行蓄洪区和滩区移民建镇工程，使40万群众远离洪水威胁
The scene of Linhuaigang Resettlement County. After the large flood in 2003, flood channels, flood storage areas and resettlement projects were constructed, keeping 400 thousand of population away from the flood threat

③ 淮河入海水道分泄洪水
The flood was discharged from the waterway of Huaihe River to the sea

④ 王家坝分洪闸分泄洪水
The flood was discharged from the flood diversion gate of Wangjiaba Dam

⑤ 洪泽湖大堤
Hongze Lake embankment

⑥ 石漫滩水库调洪错峰，充分发挥防洪效益
The Shimantan Reservoir fully playing the function of flood control by regulating the peak flood water

## 2007: Scientific Management of Flood on the Huaihe River

The whole Huaihe River basin in 2007 was faced with another large flood since 1954. At 11 o'clock of July 10, 2007, the water level of Wangjiaba Reservoir, a representative abserving location for flood on Huaihe River, reached 29.38 m, exceeding the one for flood diversion approved by the State Council by 0.08 m. At that time, there were about 150 dangerous cases in Henan province, the upper stream of Wangjiaba Reservoir, water level of Hongru River exceeded the dependable one, and those of Zhengyangguan and Hongze Lake were also rising. The situation was serious.

To divert the flood or not? Under this circumstance, the State Flood Control and Drought Relief Headquarters made the decision of lifting the gate of Wangjiaba Reservoir, and discharging the flood water to the Mengwa detention area in accordance of the rainfall data analysis. The scientific decision helped control the flood. On July 11, 2007, the flood peak of the Huaihe River's main stream went through the Wangjiaba Reservoir, and the flood flows away as expected. The flood caused the displacement of a population of 800 thousand. There was no death, no break and no dam-failure.

The scientific management of Huaihe River in 2007 expressed the practice of the concept of putting people first and the harmony between human and water, and giving the way out for flood water. Currently for water management, attention should be paid not only to the dam strengthening and reservoir construction to control the flood, but also to the return of the river/lake banking areas and resettlement of people and relocation of towns so as to give the way out for the flood water. Although the flood diversion to Mengwa detention area caused the submerging of 180 thousand *mu* of cultivated lands and resettlement of 3,684 local people, it brought about the safety of more people and protection of the big cities, factories and communication lines along the Huaihe River.

## ◆ 干旱灾害防御
## Prevention and Resist of Droughts

我国每年遭受各种自然灾害的农田面积和作物减产损失中，旱灾占一半以上，严重制约着我国农业持续、稳定、健康发展。严重的旱灾还影响城乡供水、工农业生产和生态环境，给国民经济和社会发展造成重大损失。

党和政府十分重视防旱抗旱减灾工作，兴修大量水利工程，全国水利工程实际供水能力达7491亿立方米，有效灌溉面积达8.77亿亩，抗旱能力有了显著提高。同时，积极推进抗旱应急水源工程建设，因地制宜地开展小型农田水利工程建设，提高了农业综合生产能力。全国建立了县级抗旱服务队1848个，乡镇级抗旱队9038个。目前，我国已初步建立全国旱情监测、预报和抗旱指挥决策支持系统，遇到中等干旱年份，可以基本保证城乡供水安全，工农业生产和生态用水不会受到大的影响。1991年以来，全国平均每年抗旱浇地4.46亿亩，年均挽回粮食损失4059万吨，平均每年解决2486万人的临时饮水困难。

The losses of cultivated lands and reduction of crops were caused by natural disasters and over half of it from the drought, which constrains the sustainable, stable and healthy development of agriculture. The serious drought also impacts the urban and rural water supply, industrial and agricultural production as well as the ecosystem, causing great loss to the economic and social development.

The Central Government attaches great importance to the drought mitigation work. The construction of lots of water projects helps improve the water supply capacity to 749.1 billion $m^3$, and achieve 877 million *mu* of effective irrigated lands, thus improving remarkably the drought relief capacity. Meanwhile, the water sources projects and small rural water projects have been constructed to improve the comprehensive production capacity. There are 1,848 drought relief teams at the county level and 9,038 teams at the town level. At present, the national drought monitoring, forecasting and decision supporting system has been Shaped. Therefore, at the moderate drought years, less impact will be produced on water supply, industrial and agricultural production as well as the ecosystem protection. Since 1991, 0.446 billion *mu* of cultivated lands have been benefited from irrigation each year, which saved 40.59 million tons of food production annually. And 24.86 million of population have gained the access of safe drinking water each year.

① 甘肃景泰川电力提灌工程
　　Jingtaichuan Electric Pumping Irrigation Project in Gansu Province
② 广西凤山县地头水柜
　　Water tank in Fengshan County, Guangxi Zhuang Autonomous Region
③ 宁夏固海地区扬黄干渠长山头渡槽
　　Changshantou Aqueduct in Guhai Irrigation District, Ningxia Hui Autonomous Region
④ 河南郑州市邙山提灌站
　　Mangshan Pumping Irrigation Station, Zhengzhou City, Henan Province

①

②

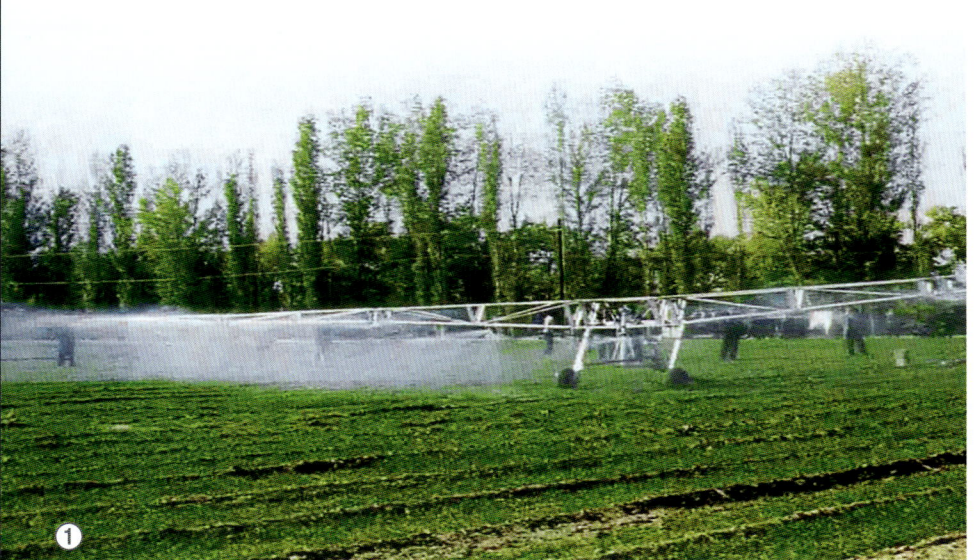

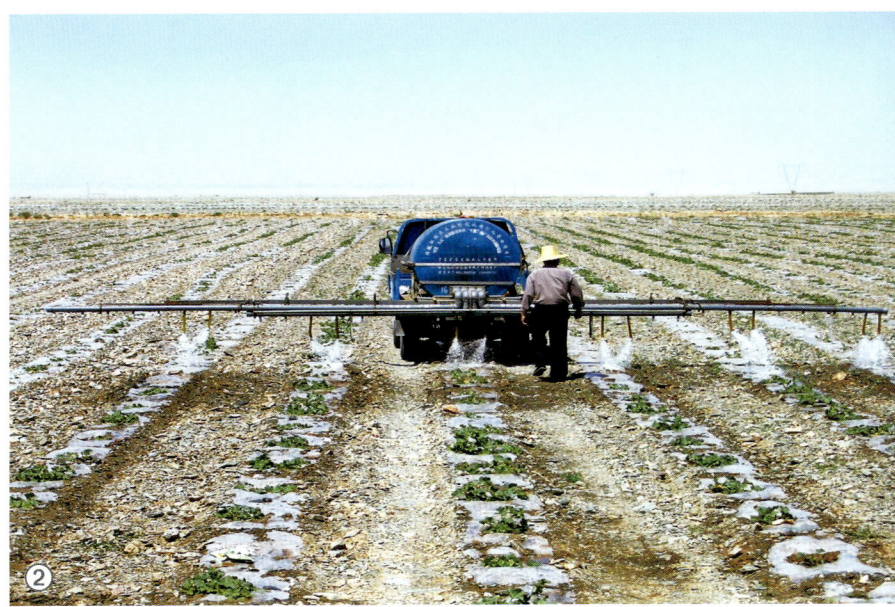

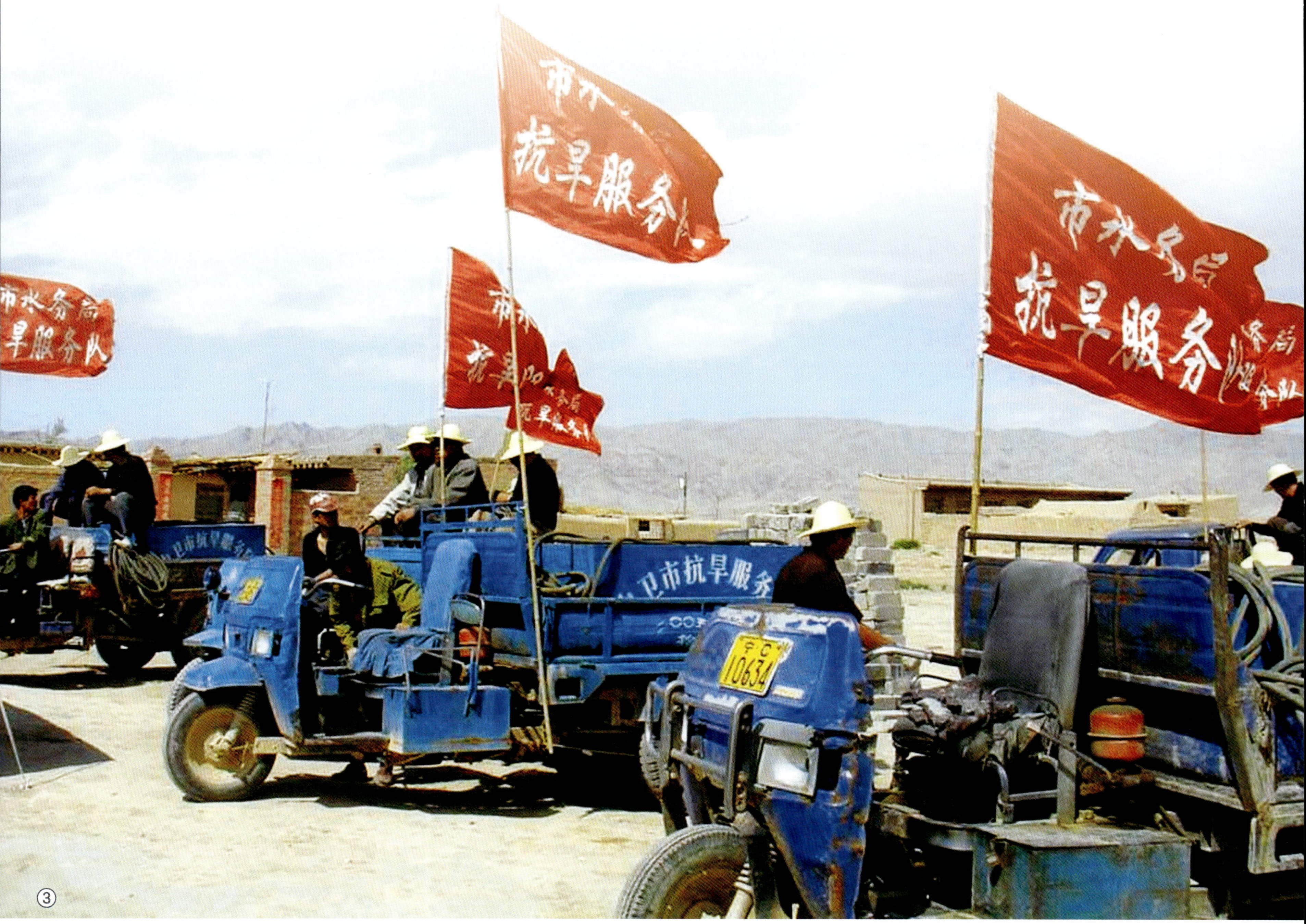
市水务局
抗旱服务
卫市抗旱服务
宁G 10634
③

① 干旱地区规模化灌溉技术
　　The large-scale irrigation techniques in arid areas
② 抗旱保苗
　　Drought relief for seedlings
③ 宁夏中卫市水务局抗旱服务队拉水抗旱
　　Carrying water for drought relief by the service teams of water affairs, Water Bureau of Zhongwei City in Ningxia Hui Autonomous Region
④ 海南抗旱井
　　Drilling a well for drought relief in Hainan Province
⑤ 开凿应急抗旱水源井
　　The department of water resources organized the drilling of emergency wells for drought relief
⑥ 重庆水利部门为群众送水
　　Service teams of drought relief delivered water in Chongqing City

① 为了缓解北京市水资源紧缺状况，保证首都供水安全，水利部门从2003年起多次组织实施了从山西册田水库向北京集中输水

To ease up the water shortage in Beijing city and secure water supply for the city, the MWR has organized implementation from water transfer from Cetian Reservoir in Shanxi Provine since 2003

② 为了解决天津市的缺水危机，从2000年起水利部门组织实施了多次引黄济津应急调水，保障了天津市居民用水安全和社会稳定

To solve the problem of water shortage in Tianjin City, the MWR has implemented several emergency water diversions from the Yellow River to Tianjin City since 2000, which ensures the water safety and stability of Tianjin City

③ 甘肃旱区实施大型灌区续建配套与节水改造，灌区面貌大为改善

The problem of water shortage has been largely relieved in the arid zone of Gansu Province after the provision of supporting facilities and water saving renovation for large irrigation districts

④ 被邓小平同志誉为"第二个都江堰"的四川省武都引水工程控灌耕地400余万亩，直接灌溉农田228万亩，400余万人受益

Wudu Water Diversion Project in Sichuan Province, praised by Mr. Deng Xiaoping as the second Dujiangyan with designed irrigated area of 4 million *mu*, irrigates the arable land of 2.28 million *mu* farmland and benefits more than 4 million people

Chapter III Disaster Prevention and Mitigation 第三篇 防灾与减灾

### ◆ 极端天气应对
### Counter Measures for Extreme Weather Conditions

我国是世界上遭受台风及极端天气影响最严重的国家之一。平均每年有7个台风在我国沿海登陆，最多年份可达12个，最少年份也有3个。台风暴潮不仅给沿海地区造成严重灾害，而且常常深入内陆造成江河洪水和山洪、滑坡、泥石流等次生灾害。

新中国成立前，我国海堤残破不全，系统的台风防御工作无从谈起，台风灾害频繁，灾难深重。新中国成立后，党和政府高度重视防台风工作，把确保人民生命安全放在台风防御工作的首位，紧紧围绕"不死人、少损失"的目标，突出抓好"防"、"避"、"救"三个重要环节。特别是20世纪90年代以来，加强了防台风工程措施和非工程措施建设，防御台风灾害的综合能力有了根本性的提高，实现了由被动、盲目地承受台风灾害，到全面主动、实施防御的重大转折，大大减轻了人员伤亡和灾害损失。目前，我国已建成海堤13830千米，其中重点海堤8094千米，部分地区重点建设了一批高标准的避风港、渔港，工程防护体系日益完善。

① 2009年8月6日，陈雷部长主持召开国家防汛抗旱总指挥部会商会，部署"莫拉克"台风防御工作
On August 6, 2009, Minister Chen Lei chaired the meeting at the State Flood Control and Drought Relief Headquarters on the arrangement for preventing the typhoon"Morek"

②③ 台风来袭
Typhoon was coming

④ 船只回港避风
The vessels were taking shelter from the wind in the harbor

⑤ 组织人员紧急转移
Organizing the urgent evacuation of local people

⑥ 钱塘江海塘
The Qiantangjiang Coastal Levee

④

China is one of the countries in the world suffering from the extreme weather like typhoon. In each year, 7 typhoons will be landed from the coastal areas averagely. There would be 12 typhoons at the most each year, and 3 ones at the least. The typhoon storm surge would not only bring the severe impact to the coastal areas, but also to the inland, causing the secondary disasters like flood, flash flood, landslide and mud flow.

Before the founding of new China in 1949, the sea embankments in China were old and broken. There was no complete systems to fight against typhoons. The frequent typhoon caused severe damages. Since 1949, the central government has paid great attention to the typhoon prevention work and given the priority to people's lives, focusing on the prevention, displacement and rescue to achieve the aim of "no death, less losses". Especially after the 1990s, the engineering measures were combined with non-engineering ones, helping raised the comprehensive prevention capacity and realize the change from passively and blindly enduring typhoons to actively fighting against typhoons in an all round way thus having reduced the death, injury and losses successfully. The coastal levees reached 13,830 km, among which 8,094 km were major ones. In some areas, high-standard ports and fishery harbors have been constructed resulting in the improved engineering prevention and protection systems.

⑤

⑥

2008年1月，我国南方部分地区遭遇了历史罕见的低温雨雪冰冻灾害，给城乡供水、灌溉排涝、农村水电、水文监测等水利设施造成了严重损失。面对突发的极端天气灾害，各级水利部门采取措施积极应对，千方百计保障灾区群众生活用水用电和重要部门供电，确保了水利工程的安全运行。

In January of 2008, the South China was encountered with a deep-freeze disaster seldom seen in history, which caused severe damage to the infrastructures in the field of urban and rural water supply, irrigation and drainage, rural hydropower as well as hydrological monitoring. Faced with the sudden extreme weather disaster, the water sector at all levels took vigorous actions to ensure the water and power supply for the domestic use and some important agencies and guaranteed the safe operation of water projects.

Chapter III Disaster Prevention and Mitigation 第三篇 防灾与减灾

① 冰雪袭击后的乡镇
The county hit by the ice and snow

② 水利技术人员检修水表
The water technicians were examining and repairing the water meters

③ 向居民集中供应生活用水
The unified water supply to the residents

④⑤ 水利职工全力抗击冰冻灾害
The water staffs were fighting against the deep-freeze disaster

## 水利抗震救灾
### Prevention of Earthquake Caused Water Disasters

2008年发生的"5·12"汶川特大地震是新中国成立以来破坏性最强、波及范围最广、救灾难度最大的一次地震。在这次特大地震灾害中，水利工程遭受严重破坏。据统计，这次地震造成四川、甘肃、陕西、重庆等8个省（直辖市）2473座水库不同程度损毁，822座水电站出现险情，1057千米堤防不同程度破坏，因山体滑坡阻塞江河形成了105处堰塞湖，严重威胁着人民群众生命安全。同时，供水系统大面积瘫痪，造成1000多万人发生饮水困难。

面对突如其来的特大地震灾难，在党中央、国务院的坚强领导下，水利部门举全部之力、全行业之力，紧急抽调1780名水利专家、勘测设计和工程抢险人员，调集3881台（套）大型施工机械和应急设备，全力投入水利抗震救灾工作。经过艰苦卓绝的努力，有效地防范了地震次生灾害，震损水库、水电站无一垮坝，震损堤防无一决口，堰塞湖排险创造了历史奇迹，经受了安全度汛的考验，实现了零伤亡，确保了人民群众生命安全和供水安全。

The devastating earthquake in Wenchuan, Sichuan Province on May 12, 2008 was the most serious one after the founding of the People's Republic of China in 1949, affecting the broadest area and most difficult for rescue. During the earthquake, water works had been damaged seriously. According to the statistics, the earthquake caused the damages of 2,473 reservoirs in 8 provinces or municipalities such as Sichuan, Gansu, Shaanxi and Chongqing, and damaged 822 hydropower stations and 1,057 km embankments. 105 barrier lakes formed, and the local people's lives were threatened. At the same time, the water supply system was out of operation leaving 10 million people with no access to safe drinking water.

Facing the sudden earthquake, under the strong leadership of the Central Government, the whole water sector reacted actively in earthquake relief work, mobilizing 1,780 water experts, engineers and emergency staff as well as 3,881 large construction machinery and emergency equipments. After the great efforts, secondary disasters were prevented. None of the quake-damaged reservoirs or hydropower plants collapsed, none of the dikes failed land, none of the quake-formed barrier lakes causing death or injury. What had been done on the barrier lake management created a historical miracle. The life and drinking water supply were also secured.

① 水利专家检查紫坪铺水库大坝坝面受损情况
  Water experts were investigating the damages of the dam of Zipingpu Reservoir
② 紫坪铺水库大坝经抢修解除险情
  The dam of Zipingpu Reservoir relieved from emergency after remediation
③ 水利部工作组查勘水电站受损情况
  Working group of the MWR was investigating the damages of the hydropower stations
④ 在水利部工作组指导下黄公坪电站溢流堰经爆破解除险情
  The overflow weir of Huanggongping Hydropower Station was blown up and away from the risk under the guidance of the working group of the MWR

① 水利供水抢修队紧急赶赴灾区
The emergency crew for water supply was hurrying up to the disaster area

② 水利抢险队紧急抢修震损堤防
Water rescue team was making urgent repair on dams damaged by the earthquake

③ 水利专家向唐家山堰塞湖紧急运送水情自动测报装置
Experts sent the automatic hydrological measuring and reporting equipments to the Tangjiashan Barrier Lake

④ 米-26大型直升机加紧向唐家山调运除险设备
M-26 heavy helicopter carrying equipments to Tangjiashan area

⑤ 武警水电部队紧急开挖引冲槽
Armed police were taking emergency excavation of flood discharging channel of Tangjiashan Barrier Lake

经过连续10多天的艰苦奋战,唐家山堰塞湖成功泄流,抢险取得决定性胜利
The Tangjiashan Barrier Lake was discharging water after over 10 days' hardworking

Chapter III  Disaster Prevention and Mitigation 第三篇 防灾与减灾

# 第四篇　管理与改革

新中国成立60年来,特别是改革开放以来,水利事业开始由计划经济下的运行机制向适应社会主义市场经济转变,由以社会效益为主向实现社会、经济和环境的综合效益转变,由粗放型管理向现代管理转变,水利工作进入依法治水的新阶段,水利领域各项改革不断推进,我国水利事业的发展取得了历史性成就。

# Chapter IV
# Management and Reform

Since the founding of the People's Republic of China, in particular after the adoption of opening-up and reform policy, water sector has started the transition from mechanism in planned economy to adapting to socialist market economy, from focusing on social welfare to integrating comprehensive benefits in society, economy and environment and from extensive management to modernized administration thus having entered into a new phase of managing water resources in accordance with laws. Reform policies in water sector are constantly adopted and introduced so that water development has made historical achievements.

# 水利规划
## Programming and Planning of Water Projects

水利规划是水利发展和改革的基础。新中国成立60年来，编制和实施了一大批重点水利规划，有力地推动了水利事业的发展。进入21世纪，根据科学发展观的要求，水利规划工作思路实现重大调整：把人与自然和谐作为水利规划的核心理念，把以人为本，着力解决人民群众最关心、最直接、最现实的水利问题放在水利规划的首位，把水利现代化作为水利规划的方向。

在可持续发展治水思路指导下，水利规划编制工作取得丰硕成果，七大流域防洪规划、水利发展"十一五"规划、石羊河流域重点治理规划等一批重大规划得到国务院批准。全国和流域水资源综合规划、七大流域综合规划修编取得丰硕成果，水利规划体系不断完善。水利规划不仅为大规模的水利建设提供了基础依据，保证了水利建设的科学有序实施，也发挥了规划对涉水事务的社会管理职能。

Water planning and programming is the basis of water development and reform. A large number of key water plans have been formulated and implemented since 1949, providing strong support to the development of water sector. In the 21st century, guiding principle of water planning has witnessed a tremendous adjustment: the harmony between human and nature has been the core of water planning, the priorities have been given to the human-oriented, water issues mostly concerned by people, the most related to people and most realistic for people for water planning, and water modernization is set as the direction of water planning, in line with requirement of scientific development concept.

With the guidance of principle of sustainable water governance, the fruitful results have been achieved on water plans formulation: flood control plans of seven major rivers and lakes, the 11th Five-Year Plan for Water Sector, Plan for the Rehabilitation of the Shiyang River, etc. These plans

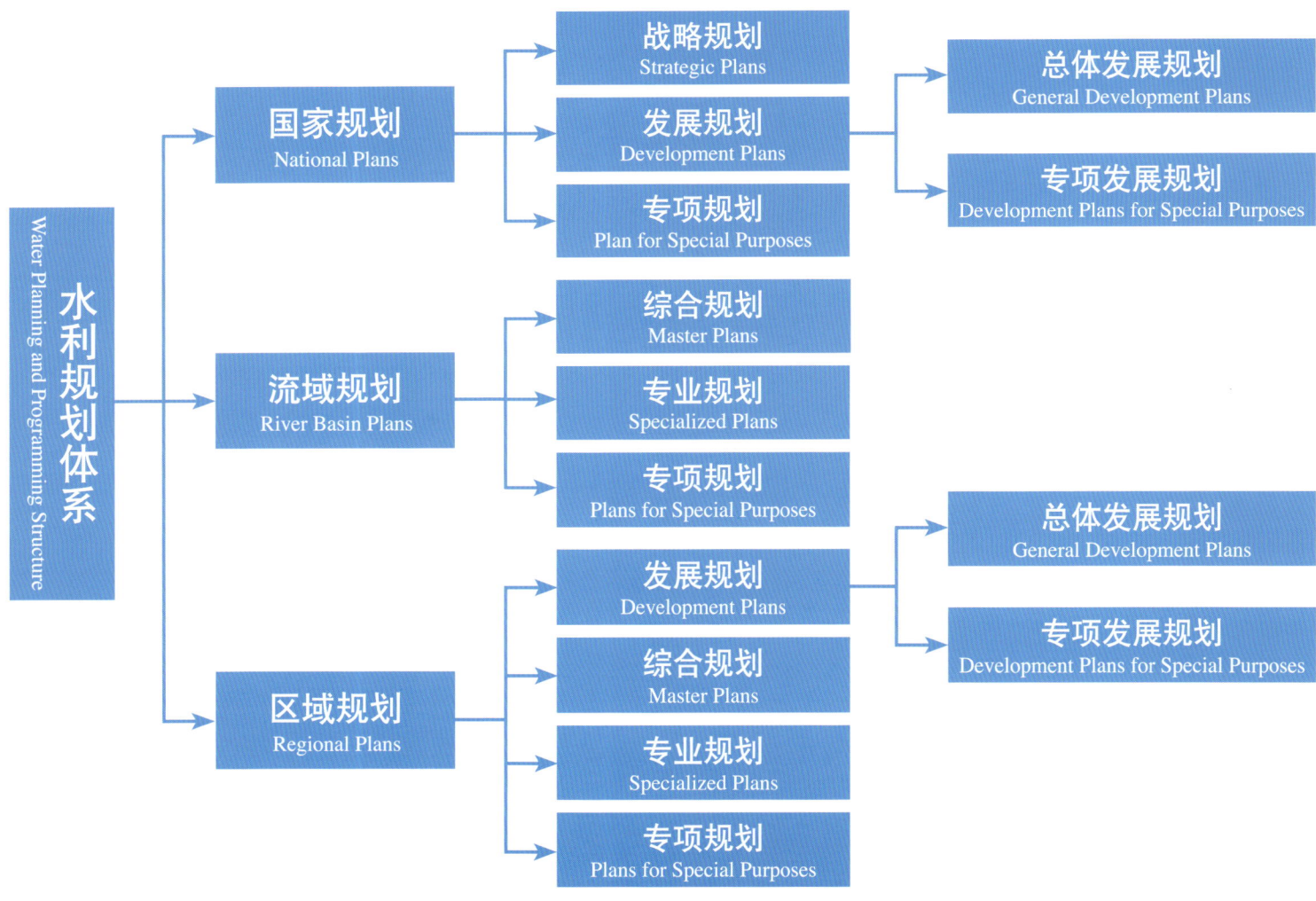

have been approved by the State Council. Much has been realized in the comprehensive planning of national and river basins' water resources, and the revision of master plan of major river basins which have contributed to a gradually improved water planning system. Water planning not only provides scientific basis, guarantees orderly implementation of water projects, but also reflects social management function upon water related issues by water planning and programming.

① 湖南皂市水利枢纽工程——水库总库容14.4亿立方米，电站总机容量12万千瓦
Zaoshi Water Project in Hunan Province with the total storage capacity of 1.44 billion m³ and the total installed capacity of 120 thousand kW

② 四川紫坪铺水利枢纽工程——水库总库容11.12亿立方米，电站总装机容量76万千瓦
Zipingpu Water Project in Sichuan Province with the total storage capacity of 1.112 billion m³ and the total installed capacity of 760 thousand kW

③ 长江流域防洪规划审查会
Review Meeting of the Flood Control Plan for the Yangtze River

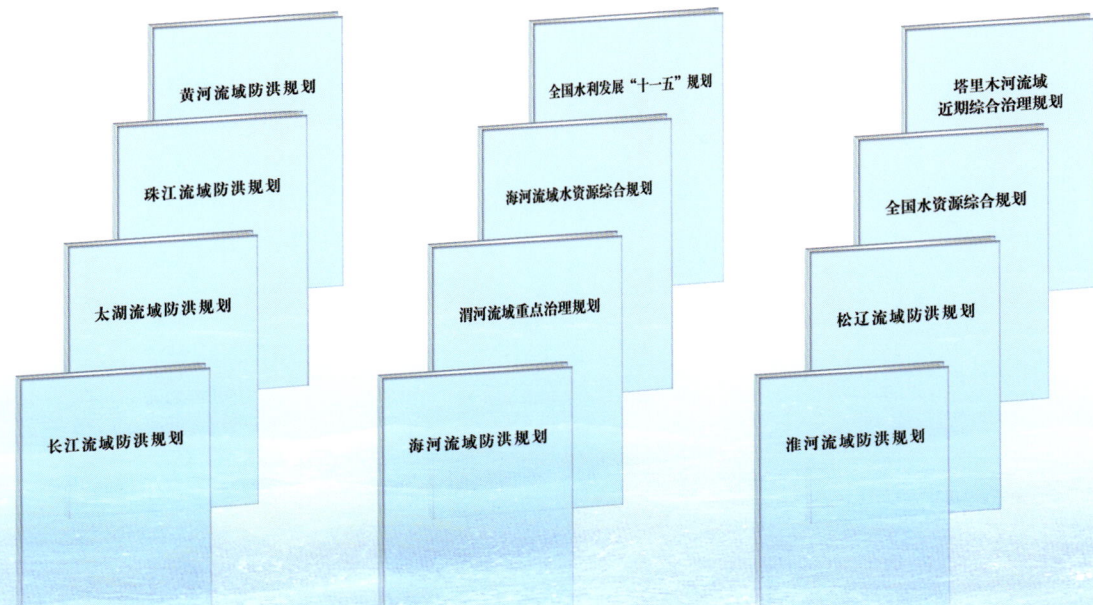

① 黄河近期重点治理开发规划
Key Treatment and Development Plan for the Yellow River in the Short-term Period

② 加强水利前期工作
Preparation for water structures

③ 甘肃省石羊河流域重点治理规划
Key Treatment and Development Plan for the Shiyang River Basin in Gansu Province

④ 宁夏黄河沙坡头水利枢纽工程——水库总库容0.26亿立方米，总控制灌溉面积134万亩，电站总装机容量12.03万千瓦
Shapotou Water Project in Ningxia Hui Autonomous Region with the total storage capacity of 26 million m³, the total irrigated area of 1,340 thousand *mu*, and the total installed capacity being 120.3 thousand kW

⑤ 石羊河中游向下游甘肃民勤县调水
　　Water diversion to Minqin County, Gansu Province from the middle reaches of the Shiyang River

⑥ 西藏满拉水利枢纽工程——水库总库容1.57亿立方米，电站总装机容量2万千瓦
　　Manla Water Project in Tibet Autonomous Region with the total reservoir storage capacity of 157 million m³ and the total installed capacity of 20 thousand kW

## ◆ 水利法治
## Legislation in Water Management

1988年《中华人民共和国水法》颁布实施，标志着我国走上依法治水的道路。几十年来，我国依法治水进程不断加快，逐步建立了以水法为核心，包括4件法律、17件行政法规、53件部规章和800余件地方性法规和政府规章的水法规体系，各类水事活动基本做到有法可依。全国成立各级水政监察队伍3400余支，专兼职水政监察人员近7万人，初步建立了覆盖全国的水行政执法网络，以行政执法责任制为重点的水行政执法制度逐步建立和完善。大力开展打击非法采砂、取缔非法取水、整治河道管理范围内非法建设、水土保持执法检查等行动，做好水事纠纷的预防调处和行政争议的化解。全面推进水利行政审批制度改革，广泛深入地开展水法制宣传教育。

The enactment of Water Law of the People's Republic of China in 1988 indicated the commencement of water management by laws. In decades, a water legislation framework with Water Law as a core has been established, composed of 4 laws, 17 administrative provisions, 53 ministerial regulations and decrees as well as over 800 local provisions and governmental regulations, and almost all water activities can be managed lawfully. 3,400 water enforcement teams have been set up with nearly 70,000 professional and concurrent staff, and a water enforcement network covering the whole country is primarily in place. The water enforcement system with responsibility of administrative enforcement is gradually set up and improved. Great efforts have been made to undertake actions

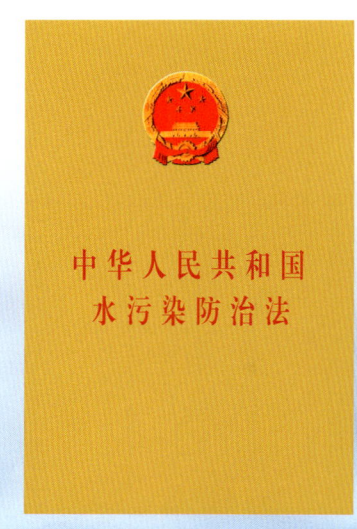

Water Law of the People's Republic of China   |   Flood Control Law of the People's Republic of China   |   Water and Soil Conservation Law of the People's Republic of China   |   Water Pollution Prevention Law of the People's Republic of China

①

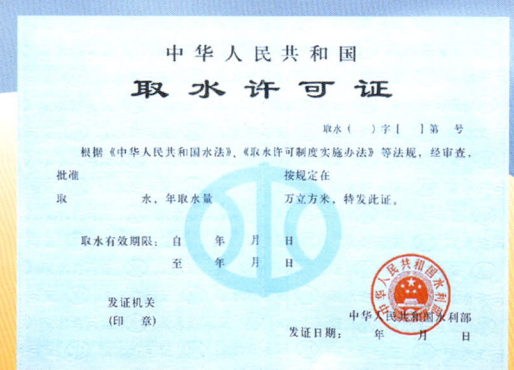

The Water Abstraction License of the People's Republic of China

②

Chapter IV Management and Reform 第四篇 管理与改革

on getting rid of illegal sediment-taking, punishing unlawful water abstraction, abolishing illegal structures within the scope of river course and checking the water and soil enforcement. Meanwhile, prevention of water disputes and addressing of administrative disagreements have been well organized. Water administrative approval system is being promoted profoundly and awareness building programs for water legislation undertaken thoroughly.

① 我国已出台的水法律
Effective water laws in China

② 依法实施取水许可
Implementing water abstraction license system

③ 九届全国人大常委会第二十九次会议于2002年8月29日修订通过新的《中华人民共和国水法》
The revision of Water Law of the People's Republic of China was approved by the 29 session of the Ninth National People's Congress on August 29, 2002

④ 宁夏开展水法规宣传活动
Water regulations dissemination in Ningxia Hui Autonomous Region

⑤ 河道采砂执法检查
Enforcement inspection for sediment-taking

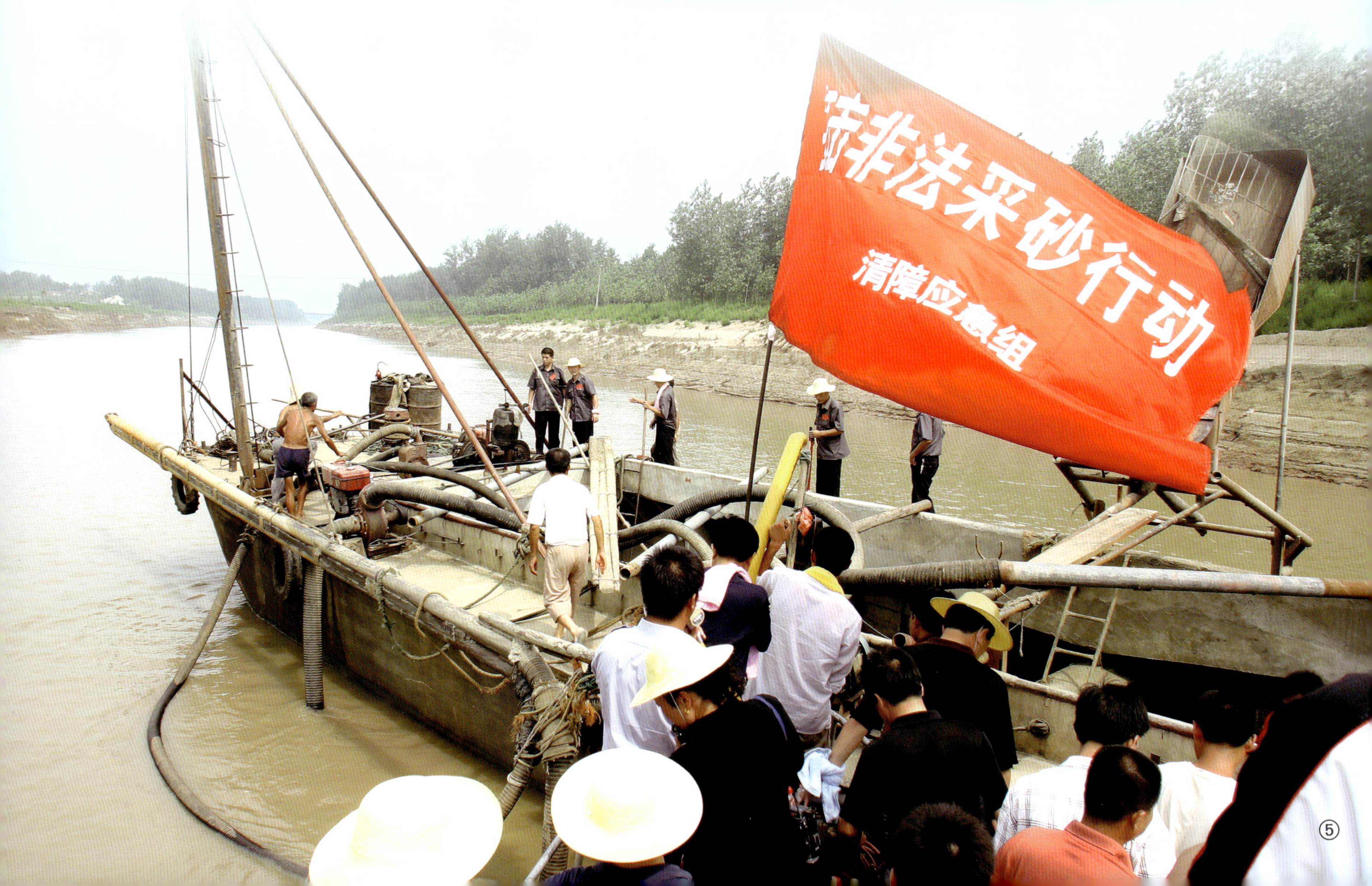

1988年以来，全国共查处水事违法案件92万起，调处水事纠纷16万多起。全国水资源统一管理的局面开始形成，取水许可、水资源有偿使用、河道采砂管理、河道管理范围内建设项目的审查等一系列管理制度普遍实施，水利法治建设为推动水利又好又快发展提供了重要的保障。

Since 1988, 920 thousand cases of water violations have been investigated and dealt with, and 160 thousand water disputes mediated. The integrated water resources management is in place, and a series of managerial provisions have been commonly applied including the water abstraction licenses, the pay-to-use water, sediment-taking management in river course and review of construction projects within the river course. Water legislation has well guaranteed the rapid development of the water sector.

Chapter IV  Management and Reform  第四篇 管理与改革

① 天津水政监察人员进行执法检查
Enforcement check in Tianjin City

② 水行政执法
Water legislation enforcement

③ 江西抚州市拆除侵占河道建筑物
Abolishing structure invading river course in Fuzhou City, Jiangxi Province

④ 解决水事纠纷,地方政府赠送锦旗
Appraisal banner is presented by local government for addressing water disputes

⑤ 水政船在珠江河口巡查
Enforcement ship patrolling at estuary of the Pearl River

## ◆ 水资源管理
## Water Resources Management

新中国成立60年来，特别是改革开放以来，针对我国经济社会快速发展与资源环境矛盾日益突出的严峻形势，党中央、国务院把解决水资源问题摆上重要位置，采取了一系列重大政策措施。进入21世纪，水利部认真贯彻中央水利工作方针，积极践行可持续发展治水思路，着力做好民生水利工作，水资源管理不断取得新的进展和突破。确立了流域管理与行政区域管理相结合的水资源管理体制，水务体制改革大力推进，取水许可、水权制度、水资源有偿使用、水资源论证、水功能区管理、入河排污口监管等一系列制度逐步建立并完善。

Since 1949, especially during the recent 30 years, the Central Committee of the CPC and the State Council have put water resources issue as top priority and taken a series of strategic policy measures in accordance with serious situation of increasing pressure imposed on resource and environment by rapid development of economy and society. In the 21st century, the MWR has actively implementing sustainable water management strategy by focusing on people with progress and breakthroughs achieved. A combined water resources management institution of river basins and administrative regions has been formed, and systems of water abstraction, water rights, pay-to-use water, water resources evaluation, water functional area management and pollutant discharge outlet supervision have been set up and improved step by step.

① 辽宁铁岭市双龙河生态建设工程
   Ecological improvement in Shuanglong River, Tieling City, Liaoning Province
② 北京转河治理
   Rehabilitation of Zhuanhe River, Beijing City
③ 地下水查勘
   Survey of groundwater
④ 城市面源污染控制技术与工程示范研究
   Research of urban non-point pollution control technology and demonstration project
⑤ 水生态修复试验
   Water ecology restoration experiment

Chapter IV  Management and Reform　第四篇　管理与改革

目前，全国七大流域管理机构初步编制完成了流域取水许可总量控制指标体系，27个省（自治区、直辖市）发布了用水定额，用水总量控制与定额管理相结合的管理制度初步建立，促进了计划用水和节约用水。31个省（自治区、直辖市）全面实施了水资源有偿使用制度。严格加强水资源论证管理，否决了一批不符合国家产业政策、高耗水、高污染的建设项目，有效遏制了水资源无序开发和过度开发。31个省（自治区、直辖市）全部完成了水功能区划，开展了水域纳污能力核定工作，提出限制排污总量。加强了入河排污口的管理，公布了118个全国重要城市饮用水水源地名录，开展了水生态系统保护与修复试点工作。全国62.9%的县级以上行政区域实行了城乡涉水事务一体化管理。

At present, seven major river basin authorities have formulated index system of total water abstraction volume control of river basin, and water use quota were published in 27 provinces, autonomous regions, municipalities and management institutions of combining total water use amount and quota management has been primarily set up, which has promoted planned water use and water conservation. Pay-to-use principle has been applied in 31 provinces, autonomous regions and municipalities. Water resources evaluation management has been strengthened, and a number of high water consumption, high pollution construction projects which do not fit for industrial policy have been rejected, effectively restraining over-exploitation and disorder in water resources development. Water function area demarcation has been completed, water pollutant load capacity reviewed and total pollutant discharge threshold proposed in 31 provinces, autonomous regions and municipalities. Management of pollutant discharge outlets are reinforced, and water source area inventory of 118 key cities are made known to the public. Pilot for water ecological system protection and rehabilitation has been started. The integrated management of water affairs has been applied in 62.9% of administrative regions at county level or above.

维持黄河健康生命
Maintain the Healthy Yellow River
河床不抬高
No Rise-up of the River Bed
污染不超标
No Violation of Legal Pollution Standard
河道不断流
No Zero Inflow in River Course
堤防不决口
No Breach of the Embankment
1 2 3 … 治理途径 … 9
Treatment Approach
原型黄河
Physical Yellow River
数字黄河
Digital Yellow River
模型黄河
Simulated Yellow River

①

饮 用 水 源 禁 止 入 内

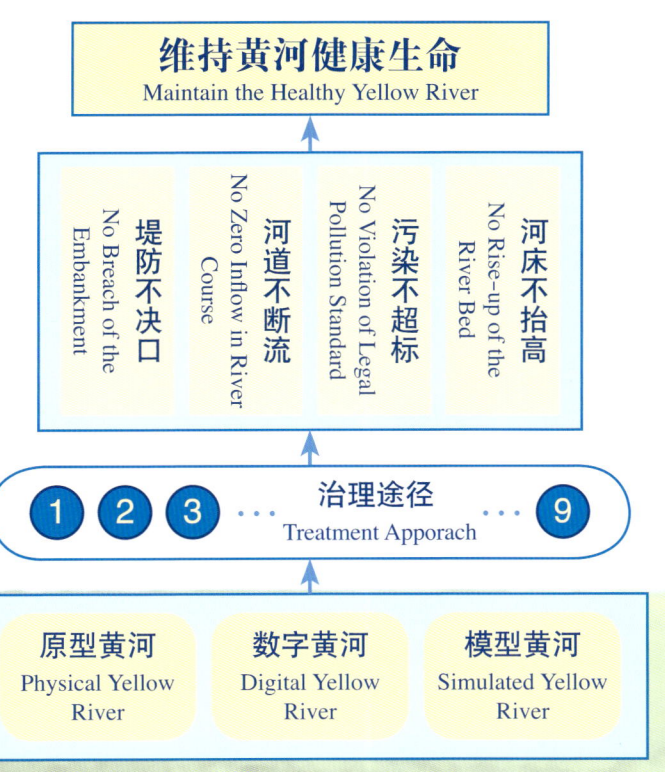

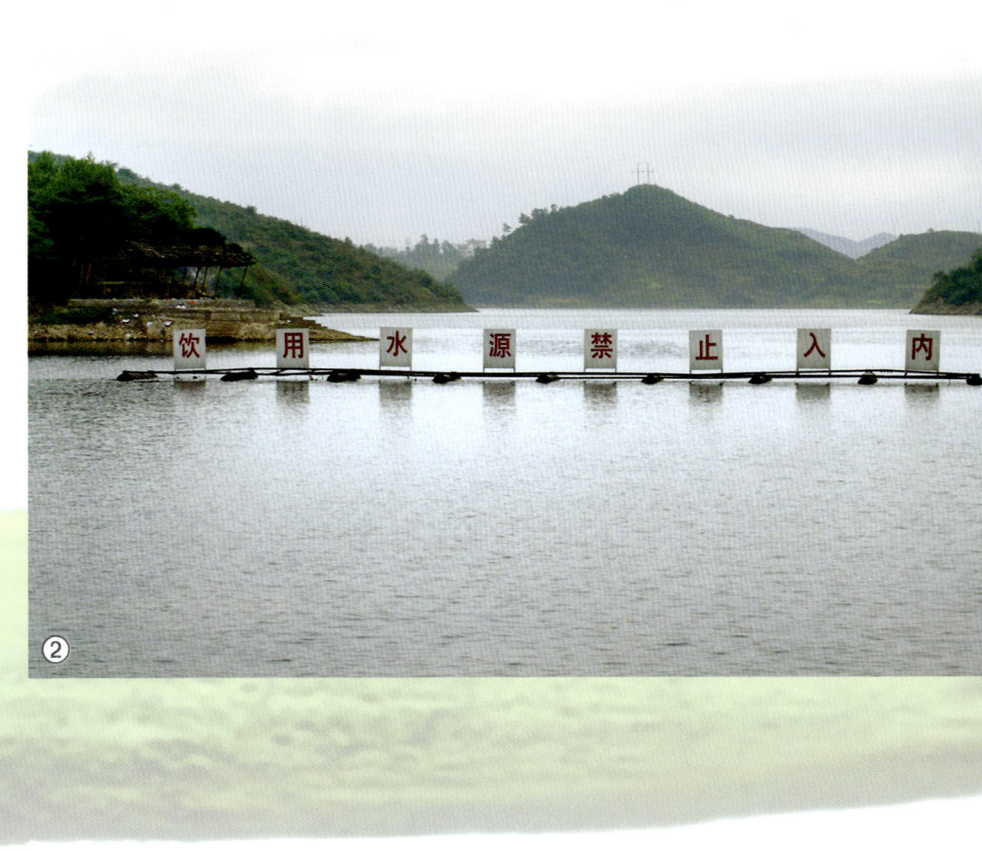

②

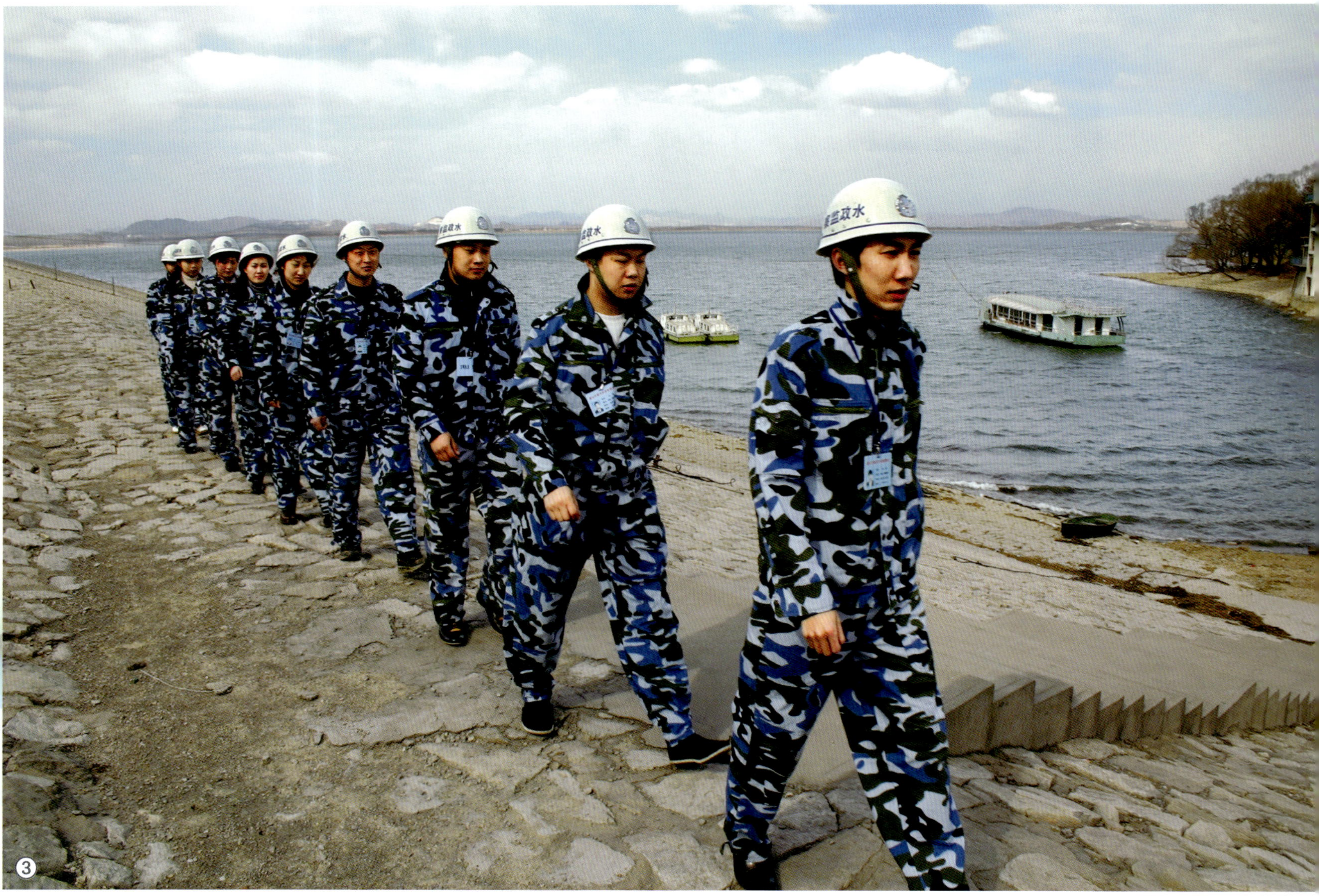

③

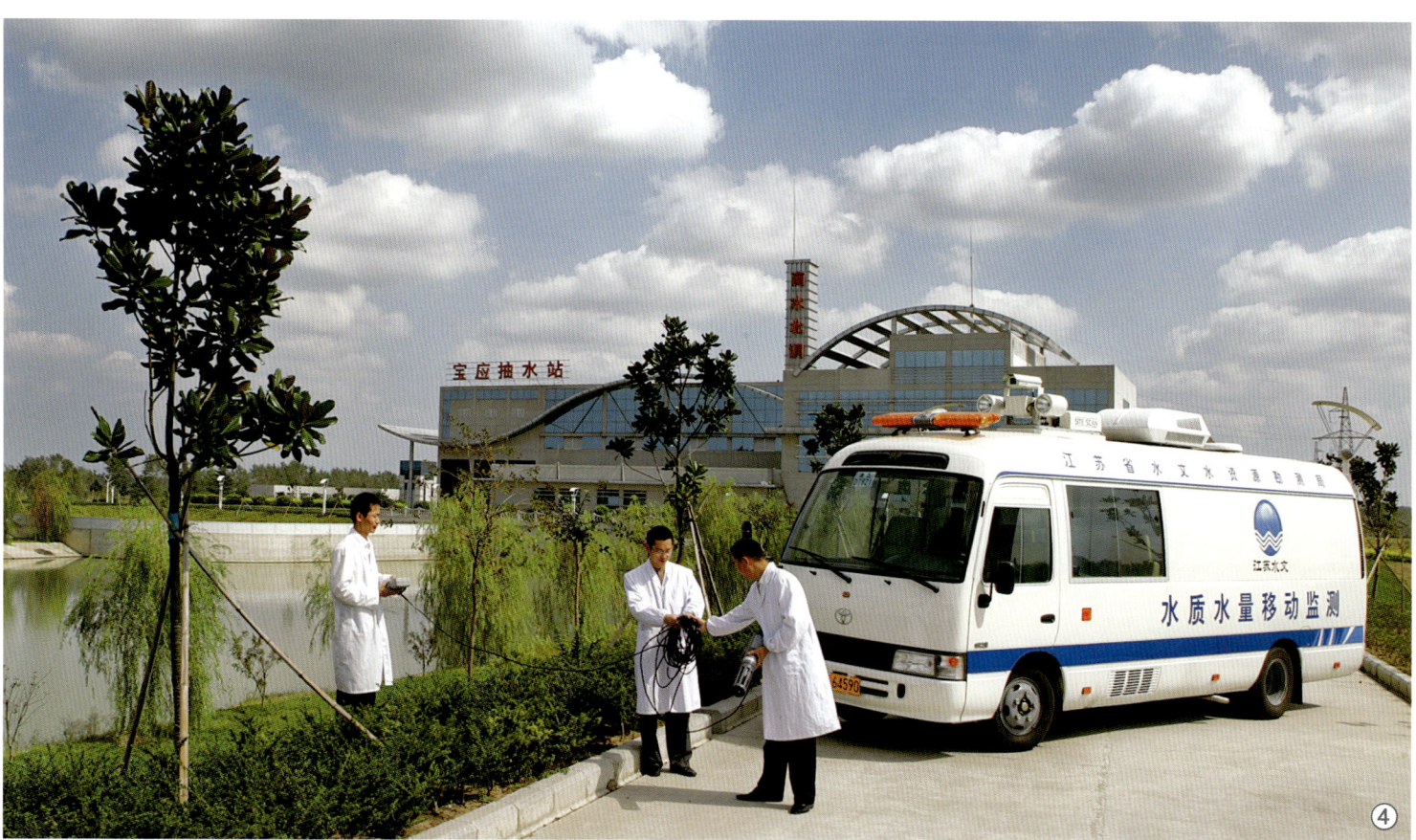

① 维持黄河健康生命理论框架示意图
Diagram of theoretic framework for maintaining the healthy Yellow River

②③ 加强水源地保护
Enforcing the protection of water sources area

④ 加强水质监测
Enforcing the water quality monitoring

⑤ 检查企业排污口
Inspecting enterprise pollutant outlet

⑥ 全国首家省水务厅——海南省水务厅2009年6月2日于海口挂牌成立
The first provincial level water affairs department established in Haikou City, Hainan Province on June 2, 2009

## ◆ 节水型社会建设
## Building of Water-saving Society

建设节水型社会是解决我国水资源短缺问题的根本性举措。近年来，水利部门稳步推进节水型社会建设，国家级节水型社会建设试点已达82个，省级试点近200个，张掖、大连、绵阳等全国节水型社会建设试点已通过验收。加快水价改革，终端水价制、超定额累进加价、丰枯季节水价、"两部制水价"等制度得到推广，农业水价综合改革全面启动，通过调整水价推动了节水。以水权水市场理论为指导，积极探索不同类型地区节水型社会建设模式和政府引导、市场调节、公众参与的运行机制。浙江东阳—义乌供水的有偿协议，宁夏和内蒙古沿黄灌区通过灌区与火电企业之间水权的有偿转让，充分体现了市场在水资源配置中的调节作用。

Water-saving society building is the fundamental measure to address water scarcity in China. In recent years, the MWR has steadily promoted the establishment of water-saving society and there have been 82 state-level pilot areas and nearly 200 provincial pilots. Pilots in Zhangye, Dalian, Mianyang, etc., have been examined. Water charge reform is under way and pricing methods of end water pricing, over-quota accumulative pricing, seasonal pricing, *two-tiers* pricing have been applied. Agricultural water pricing reform has started and water conservation is achieved by adjusting water charges. Water-saving society models in various areas and operational mechanism of government guidance, market adjustment and public participation have been explored. The trading agreement between Dongyang and Yiwu in Zhejiang Province, the paid transfer of water rights from irrigation district to thermal power plants in Inner Mongolia and Ningxia Hui Autonomous Region have reflected the adjustment role of market in allocation of water resources.

① 四川绵阳市开展节水型社会建设知识竞赛
   Water-saving society knowledge competition in Mianyang City, Sichuan Province
② 试点城市市民在"时时注意节水"横幅上签名
   Residents of pilot cities sign their names on the banner describing that water should always be conserved

我国万元国内生产总值用水量从20世纪80年代初的2909立方米降至2008年的271立方米（按2000年可比价计算），万元工业增加值用水量从953立方米下降到144立方米（按2000年可比价计算），农业灌溉水利用系数从改革开放初期的0.35提高到0.475。2000~2007年间，全国用水总量年均增幅不足1%，用水总量快速增长的趋势得到了有效遏制。

Water consumption per 10,000 *Yuan* has drastically decreased from 2,909 m³ in the early 1980s to 271 m³ in 2008 (calculated at the constant prices of 2000), and water consumption per 10,000 *Yuan* Value Added of Industry decreased from 953 m³ to 144 m³ (calculated at the constant prices of 2000). Agricultural irrigation co-efficiency has increased from 0.35 thirty years ago to 0.475. From 2000 to 2007, the increase rate of total national water consumption is less than 1% and the tendency of rapid increase of water consumption has been kept.

我国节水型社会建设试点城市和地区分布示意图
Pilot Cities and Areas of Water-saving Society Building

# 兴利除害 富国惠民 ——新中国水利60年
Generate Benefits and Mitigate Hazards to Contribute to the Prosperity of the Nation and the Interests of the People
—60 Years' Water Development in China

① 甘肃白银市灌区群众积极支持和参与灌区节水改造
The local residents in Baiyin City, Gansu Province actively support and participate in water-saving innovation of irrigation districts

② 黄河流域工农业之间水权有偿转让示意图
Diagram of water rights transfer between agriculture and industry sectors in the Yellow River Basin

从2003年开始，黄河流域进行了工农业之间的水权有偿转换实践探索，宁夏、内蒙古26个水权转换项目涉及水量2.28亿立方米

Since 2003, the water right transfer with cost has been practiced between the agriculture and industry sectors in the Yellow River Basin. In Ningxia Hui and Inner Mongolia Autonomous Regions, there are 26 such cases involving 0.228 billion m³ of water

工业项目缺水
More water needed for industry

投资引黄灌区节水改造
Investing the projects on irrigation areas (diverting water from the Yellow River) rehabilitation and water conservation

节约下来的水量用于工业项目新增用水
Water conserved for industry

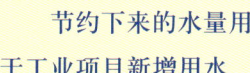

引黄灌区节水
Water conservation

③ 农民展示水权使用证
A farmer shows the water rights certificate

④ 农民查看水量分配数额
Farmers check allocated water quota listings

⑤ 农民查看用水奖罚情况公开栏
Farmers look at water use information board

① 天津梅江小区利用再生水营造和谐的人居环境
　Meijiang Community in Tianjin City creates harmonious habitat with recycled water

② 节水型社会建设试点城市张掖田园风光
　Rural landscape in Zhangye, a pilot city of water-saving society

③ 大学生生活用水使用IC卡
　Colleague students use IC card for domestic water use

④ 住宅楼楼顶集雨设施用于小区绿化
　Water collection devices (for gardening) atop of residential roofs

## ◆ 工程建设与管理
## Projects Construction and Management

新中国成立60年来，特别是改革开放以来，水利建设管理的理念、思路、体制、机制、手段和方法都发生了深刻而显著的变化，水利建设管理逐步走向法制化、规范化、科学化及现代化的轨道。水利建设领域全面推行了项目法人责任制、招标投标制、建设监理制，建立健全了质量与安全监管体系、水利建设市场主体信用体系、水利建设市场准入制度和市场监管机制，工程质量管理、安全生产管理、工程进度管理、开工和验收管理、水利建设市场监管得到进一步规范。水利工程管理体制改革加快推进，明确了公益性管理人员基本支出经费和公益性工程维修养护经费来源渠道并基本得到落实，管理体制逐步理顺，水利工程良性运行机制初步形成。

Since 1949, particularly in the recent 30 years, concept, thoughts, institution, mechanism, approach and methodology of water projects construction management have experienced in-depth and obvious changes, and water project construction management is gradually moving towards legislation, standardization, science and modernization. The responsibility system of legal person of project, system of tendering and bidding, and project supervision system have been applied in water sector, and quality and safety supervision system, credit system of construction companies, market access system and market supervision and management system have also been improved. Management of project quality, safe production, project progress, commencement, review and examination, and supervision has been specified. Management institutional reform of water projects is speeding up and sound operation environment is observed.

① 水利工程技术人员进行现场质量检测
Technicians undertaking quality check on spot

② 正在建设的黄河龙口水利枢纽工程
Longkou Water Project under construction

③ 鲁布革水电站——我国水电建设史上第一个引进外资并实行国际竞争性招标承建的重点水利工程，总装机容量60万千瓦
Lubuge Hydropower Station, the first key water project introducing foreign fund and adopting international competitive bidding in China's history of hydropower development, with total installed capacity of 600 thousand kW

④ 百色水利枢纽地下发电厂房
Underground power house of Baise Water Project

水利部门以确保质量、安全和效益为核心，牢固树立"以人为本、质量第一"的理念，坚持改革创新，坚持依法行政，坚持建管并重，坚持现代化方向，加快建设，规范管理，强化监督，全面做好水利建设与管理工作，打造了一批精品工程，为促进经济社会又好又快发展提供了强有力的水利支撑和保障。东深供水工程、淮河入海水道、临淮岗洪水控制工程、山东济南黄河标准化堤防等多项工程获得中国建设工程鲁班奖和詹天佑土木工程大奖，河南郑州黄河标准化堤防工程等42项工程获得水利工程优质（大禹）奖，全国35个工程管理单位获国家级水利工程管理单位称号。

With ensuring quality, safety and efficiency as the center, water sector has adhered to principles of "human-oriented and quality first", continued reform and innovation and paid equal attention to construction and management. A number of elite projects has been completed and provided with strong support and guarantee for the rapid development of the society and the economy. The Dongshen Water Supply Project, the Watercourse Diverting Huaihe River to the sea, the Linhuaigang Flood Control Project, and the Standardized Embankment in Ji'nan, Shandong Province, etc., have been awarded with China Construction Engineering Luban Prize (National Prime-quality Project) and China Civil Engineering Zhantianyou Prize, and 42 projects including standardized embankment in Zhengzhou, Henan Province for the Yellow River was awarded with Excellent Water Project (Dayu Award) and 35 project management agencies was awarded with national water project management units.

① 监理工程师现场检查钢筋绑扎质量
Supervision engineers checking the binding of reinforced steel bar on spot

② 新疆石门子水库大坝为目前国内最高的碾压混凝土拱坝，最大坝高109米
Dam of Shimenzi Reservoir in Xinjiang Uygur Autonomous Region is the highest RCC dam in China with the peak height of 109 m

③ 山东济南黄河标准化堤防获中国建设工程鲁班奖（国家优质工程）
Standardized Embankment in Ji'nan, Shandong Province awarded with China Construction Engineering Luban Prize (National Prime-quality Project)

④ 辽宁观音阁水库建设获得詹天佑土木工程大奖
Guanyinge Reservoir in Liaoning Province awarded with China Civil Engineering Zhantianyou Prize

⑤ 临淮岗洪水控制工程获中国建设工程鲁班奖（国家优质工程）
Linhuaigang Flood Control Project awarded with China Construction Engineering Luban Prize (National Prime-quality Project)

① 湖南江垭水利枢纽工程获国家科技进步二等奖
   Jiangya Water Project in Hunan Province was awarded with the 2nd Class National Awards for Science and Technology
② 东深供水工程获中国建设工程鲁班奖（国家优质工程）和詹天佑土木工程大奖
   Dongshen Water Supply Project for Hong Kong was awarded with China Construction Engineering Luban Prize (National Prime-quality Project) and China Civil Engineering Zhantianyou Prize
③ 淮河入海水道淮安立交获中国建设工程鲁班奖（国家优质工程）和詹天佑土木工程大奖
   Huai'an Overpass of the Watercourse Diverting Huaihe River to the Sea was awarded with China Construction Engineering Luban Prize (National Prime-quality Project) and China Civil Engineering Zhantianyou Prize

## ◆ 水文信息服务
### Provision of Hydrological Information

水文作为国民经济建设和社会发展的一项重要的基础性公益事业，是水资源进行合理开发、高效利用、综合治理、优化配置、全面节约、有效保护和科学管理的重要基础支撑。新中国成立60年来，我国的水文事业得到了长足的进步。

Hydrology is one of the important and basic pillars to support rational development, efficient utilization, comprehensive governance, optimal allocation, overall conservation, effective protection and scientific management of water resources and a basic social beneficial cause of national economic growth and social development. Since 1949, hydrological services have gained great progress.

① 20世纪80年代河北承德韩家营水文站职工用算盘计算水文资料
 Hydrologists calculating data with calculus at Hanjiaying Gauge Station, Hebei Province in the 1980s
② 20世纪60年代初，水文职工乘小舟在三门峡库区进行淤积测验
 Hydrologists conducting sedimentation experiment by boat in Sanmenxia Reservoir area in the 1960s
③ 黄河上最大的巴彦高勒大型蒸发观测站
 Large-scale evaporation observation station at Bayangaole on the Yellow River
④ 河南潢川水文站水文测验设施
 Hydrometric facilities and equipments at Huangchuan Gauge Station, Henan Province

截至2008年底，全国已建成各类水文站点37436处，其中国家基本水文站3171处、水位站1244处、雨量站14602处、水质站5668处、地下水监测站12683处，基本形成了覆盖主要江河湖库、布局较为合理、功能比较完备的水文水资源站网体系。七大江河干流水文监测能力得到明显提高。全国已有50%的雨量、水位站点实现自动观测、长期自记和数字存储。先进的流量、水质分析、泥沙测验仪器得到广泛应用。遥感、地理信息系统(GIS)、全球定位系统(GPS)等现代信息技术的应用逐步扩展。水文测报技术明显改进。建设了覆盖水利部、流域机构、省级水利部门的计算机骨干网络和异地会商视频会议系统，提高了水文信息传输的精确性和时效性。

By the end of 2008, 37,436 gauge stations of various types have been completed throughout China, out of which 3,171 are gauge stations, 1,244 are water level stations, 14,602 are rainfall stations, 5,668 are water quality stations and 12,683 are groundwater monitoring stations at national level. The layout of these stations is reasonable covering major rivers, lakes and reservoirs. The stations have formed a hydrological network with various functions. The hydrological monitoring capacity has been improved significantly. About 50% rainfall and water level stations have introduced automatic observation, long-term self-recording and digital storage. Advanced velocity, water quality analysis and sediment measuring devices have been widely applied while modern information technologies such as remote sensing, GIS, GPS have been introduced. Hydrological forecasting and measurement technology has improved. A remote visual consultation meeting system and backbone computer network connecting the MWR, river basin authorities and provincial water departments has been set up which improved accuracy of data transmission and shorten the transmission time.

据统计，我国目前每年监测收集大约6亿条水文水资源信息，至今积累了超过200亿条水文水资源信息和大量的分析研究成果。进入21世纪，水文工作围绕水资源的可持续利用和经济社会的可持续发展，服务领域不断拓宽，服务水平不断提高，在防汛抗旱减灾、水资源开发利用管理、生态与环境保护、水工程规划建设以及电力、环保、交通、航运、铁道、农业、国防等各项国民经济建设和社会发展事业中发挥了越来越重要的作用。

According to the statistics, about 600 million hydrological data are monitored and collected annually, and more than 20 billion items of water resources and hydrological data have been accumulated, acquired and stored with large amount of analysis and research results. In the 21st century, with sustainable development of the economy and the society and sustainable utilization of water resources as the center, hydrological services have explored broader areas and increased capacity playing more and more important role in flood control, drought relief, disaster mitigation, water resources management and utilization, ecological and environmental protection, water project planning and construction as well as for industries of power, environmental protection, communications, aviation, railway, agriculture and national defense.

① 水文技术人员进行水质分析
Water quality analysis

② 黄河潼关省际水质自动监测站
Automatic water quality monitoring station at Tongguan on the Yellow River

③ 黄河小北干流放淤原型观测中水文职工穿越泥滩施测地形
Hydrologists conducting geological surveys

④ 三湖河口水文站过河缆道吊箱
Cross-river cable at Hekou Hydrological Station

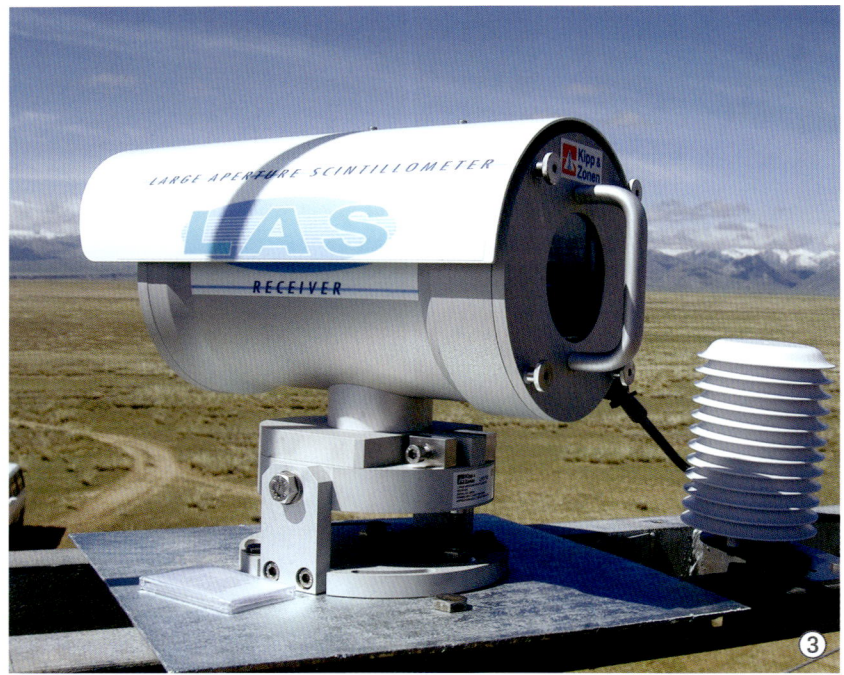

① 天津海河闸数字化水文站
Digitalized gauge station for Haihe River, Tianjin City

② 黄河温家川水文站超声波水位计
Super-sonic water-level meter in Wenjiachuan gauge station on the Yellow River

③ 黄河河源区水文自动测报装置
Automatic hydrological device at origin area of the Yellow River

④ 水文职工使用流速仪测流
Measuring velocity

## ◆ 队伍建设
## Capacity Building

水利系统不断加强党政人才、专业技术人才、经营管理人才和技能人才队伍建设，水利系统各级领导班子年轻化、知识化、专业化结构有了较大改善，科学决策、依法行政、社会管理能力和公共服务水平不断提高，干部职工的政治意识、大局意识、改革意识、服务意识不断增强。水利系统各单位不断深化干部人事制度改革，加大干部培训、交流锻炼的力度，提高了干部素质，增强了水利干部队伍的活力。职工队伍学历结构和专业结构得到改善，思想政治素质和业务素质不断提高。

Water sector has constantly conducted training activities for the administrative, professional, operational and vocational staff to build capacity and leading groups at various levels become younger, energetic and with more knowledge and professional background. Capacity of making scientific decision, managing according to laws and providing public services has been continuously improved while the awareness of reform and service of staff has been increased. Agencies in water sector have deepened personnel mechanism reform and pay more attention to capacity building and staff exchange program, energizing water staff team. Educational background and specialization structure of staff have been diversified and improved and the professional competence have also been improved.

① 水利部副司局级领导职位公开选拔竞争上岗
Open Competition to the Deputy Director General positions in the MWR
② 水利部机关公务员及在京直属单位处以上干部理论学习系列讲座
Lectures for civil servants and division chiefs
③ 全国水利系统党风廉政建设工作会议
The National Conference on the Building of the Party's Work Style and Clean Government in Water Sector
④ 离退休干部运动会
Some retired caders attending an athletic meeting

Chapter IV  Management and Reform  第四篇　管理与改革

⑤ 重庆水文职工岗位练兵
　　Hydrologist on-duty capacity building in Chongqing City
⑥ 青年水利职工在工作实践中锻炼成长
　　Young water engineers growing up in practices
⑦ 水利专家涉水渡河查看堰塞湖
　　Water experts surveying barrier lake
⑧ 南京防汛机动抢险队进行防汛演练
　　Emergency team drilling for flood control in Nanjing City

水利是一个艰苦行业，广大干部职工恪尽职守，顽强拼搏，无私奉献，表现出了良好的政治素质和精神风貌，涌现出了一大批劳动模范和先进人物。进入21世纪，在"献身、负责、求实"的水利行业精神鼓舞下，水利系统不断加强党风廉政建设和政风行风建设，重视离退休干部工作，水利精神文明建设不断向纵深拓展，先后有21个单位被评为"全国文明单位"，48个单位被评为"全国精神文明建设工作先进单位"，33个单位被评为"全国创建文明行业先进单位"，228个单位被评为水利文明单位，418个单位被评为文明灌区、文明工地、文明水文测站、文明服务示范窗口等。广大水利干部职工在抗洪抢险的危急时刻、抗震救灾的生死关头，经受了严峻考验，树立了良好形象，赢得了广泛赞誉。

Water sector features in hardworking and harsh working environment. All staff have devoted to their duties and a large number of labor models and advanced figures have merged. In the 21st century, with the guidance of the sector's spirit of "devotion, accountability and matter-of-fact attitude", and the building of the Party's work style and clean government as well as work styles of the government and the trade have been strengthened, and great attention has been paid to the works related to retired caders, and the building of the spiritual civilization in water sector has extended widely and 21 units have been labeled as "National Civilization Unit", 48 units as "National Advanced Unit for Spiritual Civilization", 33 units as "National Advanced Unit in Creating Advanced Industry", 228 units as Civilized Unit of Water Sector, 418 units as Civilized Irrigation District, Civilized Construction Site, Civilized Gauge Station and Civilized Service Division, etc. At the crucial time of do-or-die for flood control and earthquake relief, water staff has stood up to the severe tests and set up model image and gained extensive appraisal.

① 西藏水利职工野外作业
Field work of Tibetan water workers

② 水利技术人员为保证工程质量精益求精
Water technicians keep on improving the quality of their work

③ 黄河水利职工在内蒙古河段开展凌情巡测
Observing ice flood regime along the Yellow River in Inner Mongolia Autonomous Region

④ 水利技术人员在地震灾区冒着飞石滚落的危险进行勘测
Water technicians carrying out surveys at the risk of collapsing rocks

⑤ 全国"五一"劳动奖章获得者、全国抗洪模范、四川沱江登瀛岩水文站勘测工张宇仙26年如一日，在平凡岗位上谱写奋斗之歌、青春之歌

Mrs. Zhang Yuxian, the hydrological worker of Dengyingyan gauge station, Tuojiang River, Sichuan Province, awarded of National May 1st Labor Medal, National Flood Control Model, has worked in the place for 26 years

⑥ "中国工程勘察大师"、长江水利委员会综合勘测局原总工程师崔政权鞠躬尽瘁，死而后已，把毕生精力献给治江事业

Mr, Cui Zhengquan, former Chief Engineer of Comprehensive Survey Bureau of the Changjiang Water Resources Commission, and China National Engineering Survey Master, career devoted all his life till his death to the Yangtze River management

⑦ 全国"五一"劳动奖章获得者、黄河水利委员会水文局玛多水文站勘测工谢会贵在海拔4200多米的青藏高原埋头苦干30年

Mr. Xie Huigui, hydrological worker of Maduo gauge station, Yellow River Conservancy Commission, awarded of National May 1st Labor Medal, has worked in Tibet Plateau with altitude over 4,200 m for 30 years

⑧ 全国第五届"人民满意的公务员"、水利部原总工程师高安泽敬业为公、勤政为民

Mr. Gao Anze, former Chief Engineer of the MWR and the National Satisfactory Civil Servant, has been diligent for the people

⑨ 水利部长江水利委员会长江勘测设计研究院总工杨启贵（右）在2008年水利抗震救灾斗争中表现突出，被党中央、国务院授予"全国抗震救灾模范"称号

Mr. Yang Qigui, Chief Engineer of the Institute of Survey, Planning, Design and Research of Changjiang Water Resources Commission, was awarded with National Model of Earthquake Disaster Relief in 2008

⑩ 根据吉林省水利厅原厅长汪洋湖先进事迹创作的话剧《汪洋湖》在水利系统巡演，水利部原部长汪恕诚亲切接见演职人员

Performance of a modern drama, "Wang Yanghu", which is based on real story of former Director General of Jilin Provincial Water Resources Department. The actors and actresses were met by Mr. Wang Shucheng, former Minister of Water Resources

# 第五篇　科技与创新

新中国成立60年来，特别是改革开放30年来，水利系统实施科技兴水战略，大力倡导科技创新，积极利用高新技术改造传统水利，水利科技创新不断实现重大突破，水利信息化水平不断提升，水利建设与管理的整体科技含量明显提高，科技对水利发展的支撑保障作用明显增强。在防汛抗旱减灾、大江大河综合治理、水资源开发和保护、农村水利、水土保持、水利工程建设等重点领域取得了一批重大科技成果，新技术、新材料、新工艺、新方法得到广泛应用，水利科技总体水平与国际先进水平的差距不断缩小，部分领域达到国际先进水平，一些领域处于国际领先地位。国家防汛抗旱指挥系统工程、水利电子政务工程、水资源调度与管理系统、全国水土保持监测网络与管理信息系统工程、大型灌区信息化建设等一大批应用范围广、发挥作用大、具有代表性的水利业务应用系统相继投入运行，极大地丰富了水利业务工作的技术手段，有力地提升了水利建设和管理的现代化水平。

# Chapter V
# Science, Technology and Innovation

Since 1949, water sector has adopted strategy of development with science and technology and spared no efforts to promote innovation. New and hi-tech has been introduced to innovating traditional water sector and important breakthroughs have been achieved constantly. The supportive and guaranteeing role of science and technology upon water development is obviously improved. A large number of scientific research results have been made in aspects of flood control and drought relief, comprehensive management of large rivers, water resources protection and development, rural water supply, water and soil conservation and water projects construction, etc. New technologies, materials and methods have been widely applied and gap between China and international advancement in terms of science in general is becoming narrower. And in some areas, China is even in the leading position while in some other fields in the advanced level. Systems of state flood control and drought relief commanding, E-administration for the MWR, water resources regulation and management, national water and soil conservation monitoring network and information system and information system of large irrigation districts have been widely applied which have enriched approaches of water management and promoted modernization of construction and management.

## ◆ 科技创新能力
## Capacity of Science and Technology Innovation

水利行业不断创新人才开发的体制机制，优化人才成长环境，积极培养和吸引各类人才，努力创造有利于培养人才和用好人才的良好环境。目前，全国水利行业共有专业技术人员34万余人，其中具有中高级职称的有14.8万人。部属4个非营利科研院所，70%以上的科研人员具有硕士、博士学位。通过科学整合、深化改革、加强建设，水利科研机构布局得到优化，机制更加灵活，科研能力明显增强，服务领域不断拓展。我国已建立5个国家水利重点实验室和3个国家水利工程技术研究中心，6个部级重点实验室和10个部级工程技术研究中心以及一批省级重点实验室、工程技术研究中心及科研试验基地，其中灌溉试验站123个、水文实验站46个、水土保持试验站130多个。国家对水利科技的投入显著增加，多元化、多渠道、多层次的水利科技投入体系逐步形成。

Water sector constantly innovates in institution for talent development, optimizes environment for the talent, trains and educates various talent and creates sound environment for people of talent to grow up. At present, there are 340,000 professionals and technicians, out of which 148,000 possess high level professional titles. Within four non-profit research institutes, 70% researchers have degrees of masters and doctors. Through integration, reform and increasing input, research institution layout is optimized, mechanism flexible, research capacity obviously strengthened and service scope extended. Five national water laboratories and three national water engineering research centers have been set up, with also six ministerial key labs and 10 ministerial engineering research centers and provincial labs, engineering research center and experiment base for scientific research including 123 irrigation test stations, 46 hydrological test stations, 130 water and soil conservation test stations. The financial input from the state upon science has increased significantly and a diversified, multi-channel and multi-tier water research investing system is gradually formed.

① 长江干流实体模型
　Physical model of the Yangtze River

② 2008年4月1日新中国成立以来第一次全国水利科技大会召开
　The First National Congress on Water Science and Technology was held on April 1, 2008

③ 吸水速凝挡水子堤
　Dike consisting of water absorbing and quick setting material

④ 大型渠道衬砌成套装备
　Large-scale canal concrete-lining equipment

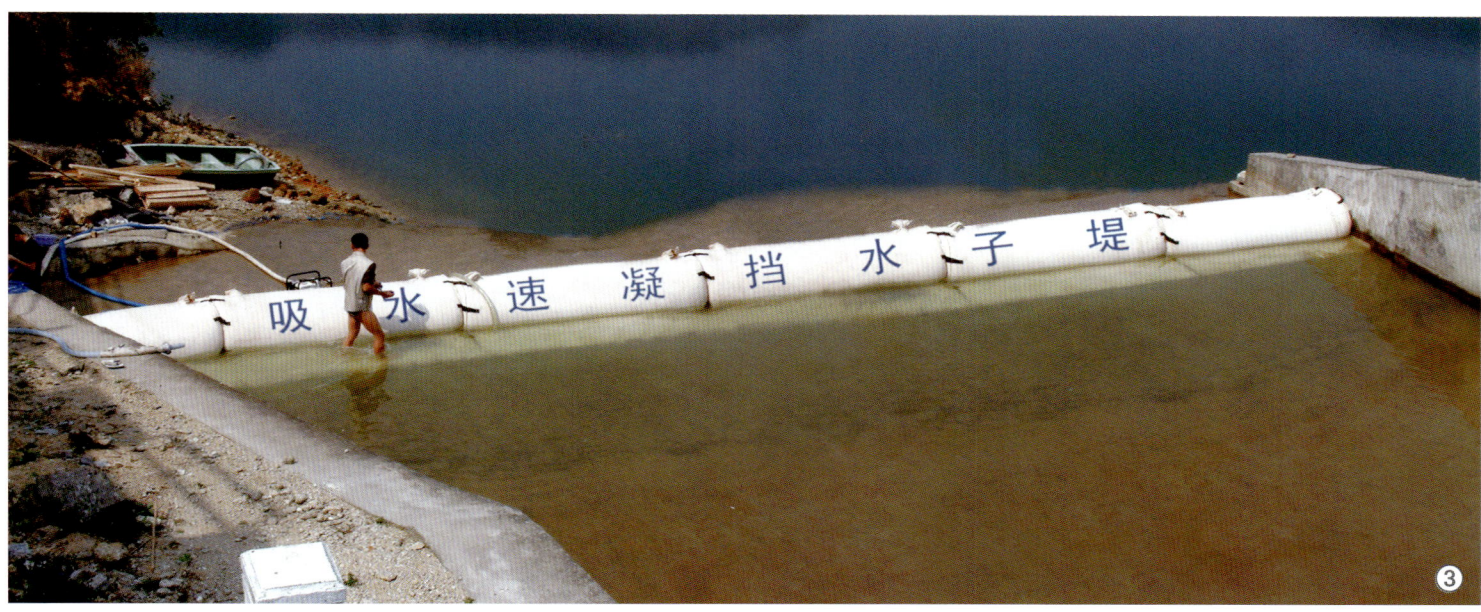

① 黄河万家寨水利枢纽物理模型模拟泄流
　Discharging simulation of physical model of the Wanjiazhai Water Project on the Yellow River
② 微喷灌溉试验场
　Experiment field of micro and sprinkler irrigation technology
③ 深圳南山区水土保持生态园水土流失模拟设施
　Simulation facilities of water and soil loss in water and soil conservation park, Nanshan District, Shenzhen City, Guangdong Province

④ 浙江金华水土保持结合低丘红壤开发
Water and soil conservation with red soil development in Jinhua City, Zhejiang Province

⑤⑥ 我国水利工程师在国外接受培训
Chinese water engineers taking overseas training program

## ◆ 重大科技成果
## Important and Significant Achievements

水利行业积极开展原始创新、集成创新和引进消化吸收再创新，重大优秀科研成果不断涌现。"十五"以来，水利系统共完成国家和部级科技项目600余项，其中33项达到国际领先水平，165项达到国际先进水平。获得国家级科技奖励46项，省部级科技奖励500余项。

在基础理论研究方面，"天然—人工"二元水循环模式、水资源合理配置理论与方法、洪水管理战略、生态水工学、分区域生态用水标准，以及中国水旱灾害研究、黄河流域水资源演变规律研究等应用基础研究取得重大进展。

在防汛抗旱减灾方面，从预测预报预警、信息采集，到指挥调度、防汛抢险，广泛采用了先进的科学技术，显著提高了防灾减灾的能力和水平。

在大江大河综合治理方面，针对不同江河的突出问题，加强科学实验，积极推广使用新技术、新材料、新工艺；黄河调水调沙、小北干流放淤等重大科学试验和研究，加快了黄河水沙失衡问题的解决步伐；长江中下游干流堤防建设广泛采用了堤防防渗加固、隐患探测的新技术，实现了工程建设质的飞跃。

① 三峡工程双线五级船闸
Permanent two-way five-grade ship locks of the Three Gorges Project

② 黄河小北干流放淤试验
Experiment of silt differentiation with gate and canal at Xiaobeiganliu on the Yellow River

The water sector actively carries out primary innovation, integrated innovation and re-innovation after introduction and digestion so that many excellent and important scientific and technological research results were brought out constantly. Since the Tenth Five-year Plan period, water sector has finished more than 600 state and ministerial scientific research programs with the results of 33 programs having reached world leading level and that of 165 programs reached international advanced level. These programs have received 46 state-level scientific awards and 500 ministerial and provincial-level awards.

In the field of basic theory research, the applied theoretical researches including "Natural-Artificial" Water Cycle Mode, Theory and Methodology of Rational Allocation of Water Resources, Flood Management Strategy, Ecological Hydro-engineering, Ecological Water Demand Standard for Various Regions, Water and Drought Disaster Research and Research on Water Resources Evolution Rule in the Yellow River Basin have made great progress.

In the field of flood control, drought relief and disaster mitigation, the advanced scientific technologies have been extensively used in forecasting, foreseeing, warning, data acquisition, commanding and emergency actions and have tremendously improved capacity of disaster prevention and relief.

In the field of integrated management of large rivers, the priority has been given to the scientific experiments for different key issues, and the state-of-the-art technologies, materials and methodologies have been promoted. The research projects of water regulation and sediment flushing experiment in the Yellow River, the sediment differentiation with gate and channel experiment in Xiaobeiganliu on the Yellow River have speeded up in addressing water and soil erosion. The embankment anti-seepage reinforcement and dike danger detecting devices have been applied in the embankment construction in the middle and lower reaches of the Yangtze River contributing greatly to the quality.

在水资源节约和保护方面，水资源承载能力评价方法的研究和应用，水权水市场理论的确立和实践，新型节水技术及设备的开发和推广，推动了节水型社会建设。水功能区划与水资源保护理论、河流生态修复技术方法、节水农业等应用技术得到广泛运用。

在农村水利方面，通过改造传统灌溉技术和设备，优化灌区水资源配置，开展全国水土保持监测网络和信息系统建设，推广应用农村水电新技术、新产品，加快了农村水利的现代化进程。

在水利工程建设方面，采用全断面岩石掘进机施工技术、盾构技术、超大型预冷强制式混凝土拌和楼等先进技术和装备，极大地提升了水利工程施工的现代化水平。三峡工程枢纽布置与船闸设计、小浪底工程孔板消能泄洪洞设计、高面板堆石坝设计施工等工程技术取得了突破性成果，我国已具备了建设世界一流水利工程的能力和水平。

① 浙江省临海市洛河曲柔护岸
Embankment protection in Linhai City, Zhejiang Province

② 世界上同类型最大的预应力混凝土U型薄壳渡槽
The largest-scale two-way pre-stressed concrete U-shape and thin shell aqueducts

③ 超大型预冷强制式混凝土拌和楼
Super large-scale forced pre-cooling concrete batching plant

④ 全断面岩石掘进机
All Section Rock TBM

⑤ 三峡工程五级船闸人字门
Twin plain gates of permanent five-grade ship locks of the Three Gorges Project

⑥ 利用世行贷款建设的小浪底工程输水隧洞
Water channels of the Xiaolangdi Water Project built with the World Bank loan

In the field of water resources conservation and protection, the research and application of evaluation approach of water resources load capacity, establishment and practice of water rights and water market theory, development and promotion of new water-saving technologies and equipments have all helped moving the water-saving society forward. The water functional areas demarcation and water resources protection theory, river restoration technology and water-saving agricultural measures have been widely put into practice.

In the field of rural water supply, irrigation and drainage, modernization process has been stridden by innovating traditional irrigation technique and equipments, optimizing water distribution in irrigation districts, extending water and soil conservation supervision network and information system and promoting the application of new technologies and products for rural hydropower.

In the field of project construction, the introduction of all section rock TBM, shield tunneling and super large-scale forced pre-cooling concrete batching plant, etc. have significantly improved construction of water projects. The breakthrough has been achieved in layout and ship lock design of the Three Gorges Project, design of hole-plate orifice dissipation tunnels and design and construction of high concrete faced rockfill dam, etc, and China has the capacity and competence for the construction of projects with the advanced level in the world.

黄河小浪底工程调水调沙
Water and sediment regulation at Xiaolangdi Project on the Yellow River

Chapter V  Science, Technology and Innovation  第五篇  科技与创新

## 技术引进推广
## Promotion and Extension of New Technologies

"十五"以来，按照技术引进、合作研究、消化吸收、创新推广相结合的技术路线，通过实施引进国际先进水利科学技术计划（水利部"948"计划），引进了500余项适合我国水利行业特点的先进实用技术，对缩短我国水利科技与世界先进水平的差距发挥了重要作用。

通过实施国家农业科技成果转化资金项目、水利部重点科技成果推广计划和地方科技推广计划，约500项先进实用的水利科技成果得到成功转化，在防灾减灾、农业高效用水、水土保持、水利工程建设等各个领域发挥了积极作用。全国已建成300余个农业节水示范地区（市）、25个部级水土保持科技示范园、140余个科技推广示范基地（园区），水利科技推广与技术服务体系的建立，取得了显著的经济效益、社会效益和环境效益。

Since the 10th Five-Year Plan Period, through introducing technology, cooperative research, digestion and innovation and promotion, more than 500 advanced practical methodologies fitting for features of water sector have been introduced by implementing the Program of Introducing Advanced Water Technologies (948 Program), which have made great input in reducing the gap of water science and technology level between China and advanced world level.

By implementing State Agricultural Scientific Output Transition Fund Program, the MWR's Promotion Plan for Key Scientific Outcomes as well as provincial science promotion plan, about 500 practical and advanced water scientific research results have been successfully applied for disaster prevention and mitigation, high-efficiency water utilization in agriculture, water and soil conservation and water projects construction, etc. More than 300 agricultural water-saving pilot areas, 25 ministerial level water and soil conservation demonstration parks and 140 science and technology promotion bases have been set up. The establishment of water science and technology promotion and service system has generated significant economic, social and environmental benefits.

① 开展中英合作小流域管理项目
　Sino-UK cooperated project on small watershed managment
② 开展中英水资源需求管理项目
　Sino-UK cooperated project on water resources demand managment

Chapter V Science, Technology and Innovation  第五篇　科技与创新

③ 堤防隐患探测技术
　Dike danger detecting equipment and technology

④ 苦咸水改良技术设备
　Equipment to improve bitter and brackish water

⑤ 贵州龙里县水土保持科技园
　Water and soil conservation park in Longli County, Guizhou Province

⑥ 举办2008年度国际水利先进技术（产品）推介会
　Holding Promotion Conference on International Advanced Water Technologies

## ◆ 国际合作交流
### International Exchanges

我国水利部门以积极的姿态参与涉水国际组织与重大国际水事活动，深入开展以技术合作为重点、辐射水利政策和管理各个领域的水利交流与合作，形成了全方位、多层次、宽领域的对外开放格局，在推动中国水利全面登上国际舞台，加快水利基础设施建设，扩大水利技术、设备输出，增强国际竞争力等方面发挥了重要作用。

近年来，国际大坝会议、国际水土保持大会、国际灌排大会等有影响的国际水利会议在我国举办，黄河国际论坛、长江论坛等我国水利行业发起的国际会议在世界上的影响力越来越大，世界水论坛、亚太水峰会、新加坡国际水周等一些重要的国际水事活动纷纷邀请中国代表作特邀报告或主旨发言，我国一批优秀水利专家在国际大坝委员会、国际小水电组织、国际灌溉排水委员会等重要的国际组织中担任要职。

The water sector in China has been actively involved in the important international water-related events and cooperated with the international water organizations. With technical cooperation as the focus, the exchanges and cooperation covering various areas such as policies and management have been carried out forming an overall, multi-level, broad areas and opening up framework contributing to advancing to the international arena, speeding up water infrastructure construction, expanding export of water technology and equipment, and increasing international competitiveness, etc.

In recent years, China has held influential international meetings, including ICOLD Congress, International Conference on Water and Soil Conservation and ICID Conference, etc. The international events such as the Yangtze River Forum and the Yellow River International Forum initiated by Chinese water agencies have gained more and more acknowledgement. For the important international forums including World Water Forum, Asia Water Summit and Singapore International Water Week, the Chinese delegates have always been invited to present special reports or deliver keynote speeches. Some outstanding water professionals from China have held important positions in international water organizations.

① 水利部部长陈雷在土耳其召开的第五届世界水论坛作主旨发言
Mr. Chen Lei, Minister of Water Resources, delivered a keynote speech at the 5th World Water Forum held in Istanbul, Turkey

② 第九次河流泥沙国际学术讨论会在我国举办
The Ninth International Symposium on River Sedimentation held in China

③ 长江论坛
The Yangtze River Forum

④ 黄河国际论坛
The Yellow River International Forum

改革开放以来，我国水利行业利用外资累计已达70多亿美元。黄河小浪底水利枢纽等一大批水利重点项目利用外资得以及时兴建。通过实施亚行贷款松花江洪水管理项目、中瑞长江洪水预报项目、全球环境基金（GEF）海河流域水资源与水环境综合管理等一批重大国际科技合作项目，学习了国外先进技术和管理经验，加强了行业能力建设。

我国水利部门以技术优势开展同发展中国家的合作，积极开拓国际市场。水电站机电设备、小水电设备、防渗材料、雨水集蓄利用等先进设备和技术的出口规模不断扩大，对外技术咨询业务量不断增加；在小水电、土壤侵蚀与泥沙防治、雨水集蓄利用等领域，举办了一系列国际培训班，为发展中国家培训了大量技术人才。

目前，我国水利机构和专家已参加了40多个政府间和非政府间国际水利组织；在我国成立了国际小水电中心、国际泥沙研究培训中心等，为南南合作作出了积极贡献。我国水利行业已同60多个国家或地区建立了合作关系，与近40个国家签订了科技、经济合作协议或谅解备忘录，水利国际合作与科技交流的领域不断拓展。

Since the adoption of the reform and opening-up policy, water sector in China has accumulatively utilized more than 7 billion US dollars and a great number of key water projects have been completed with overseas fund such as Xiaolangdi Multi-purpose Dam Project. By implementing a large number of international cooperative projects including the ADB-funded Songhua-Liaohe River Flood Management Project, the Sino-Switzerland Yangtze Flood Forecasting Project and GEF-funded Haihe River Water Resources and Water Environment Integrated Management Project, the advanced technologies and managerial experience and concepts have been introduced into China and helped strengthen the capacity building of the sector.

① 埃塞俄比亚水电站技术人员在我国接受培训
Ethiopian hydropower station engineers taking training in China

② 我国水利企业参与建设的马来西亚巴贡水电工程
The Bakun Hydroelectric Project in Malaysia constructed by Chinese company

③ 雨水集流国际培训班学员考察集雨农业示范园区
Trainees from International Rainwater Collection Training Course visiting rain-fed agricultural demonstration area

④ 尼日利亚水利同行在甘肃定西考察水窖建设
Nigerian engineers learning water tank in Dingxi City, Gansu Province

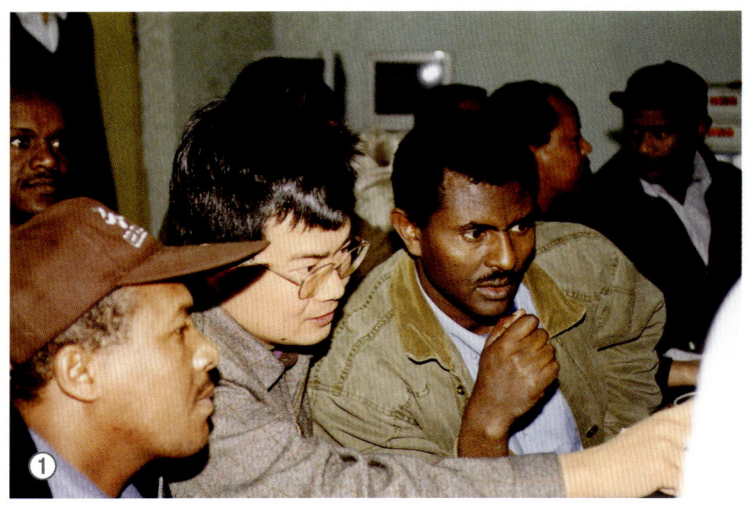

Water agencies undertake cooperation with developing countries with technological advantage and positively explore international market. The export of electrical units and system, small hydropower equipments, water-proofing material, rain-water collection technology has constantly increased, as well as the overseas consulting tasks. A series of international train courses have been held in China for small hydropower, soil erosion and sediment prevention, rain-water collection, etc. to train a great deal of engineers and technicians for developing countries.

At present, Chinese water agencies and experts have joined over 40 inter-governmental and non-governmental organizations, and have set up International Center on Small Hydropower, International Center for Sediment Research and Training, etc., making great contribution to South-South Cooperation. Chinese water sector has established cooperative relationship with more than 60 countries and regions, and signed scientific, economic cooperation agreements or MOUs with nearly 40 countries, and the scope of water international cooperation and exchange has been continuously extended.

⑤ 水利部部长陈雷与哥斯达黎加环境与能源部部长多布莱斯签署水资源领域合作谅解备忘录
Mr. Chen Lei, Minister of Water Resources, signed a cooperative MOU on water resources with Mr. Roberto Dobles, Minister of Environment and Energy, Costa Rica

⑥ 水利部部长陈雷与世界水理事会主席洛克·福勋签署合作谅解备忘录
Mr. Chen Lei, Minister of Water Resources, signed a MOU with Mr. Loic Fauchon, President of World Water Council

## ◆ 水利信息化
### Information Technology

我国水利信息化工作起步于20世纪70年代中后期，近年来水利系统坚持以水利信息化带动水利现代化，初步形成了由基础设施、应用系统和保障环境组成的水利信息化综合体系，计算机通信网络技术得到广泛应用，实现了基础数据的自动化全天候实时获取、传输、存储和处理，水文基础数据库建设加快，水利信息公众服务能力明显增强，有力地推动了传统水利向现代水利、可持续发展水利转变。

全国省级以上水利部门已建成各类信息采集点约2.7万个，其中自动采集点占47.5%，信息采集的精确性、时效性、有效性以及工程监控的自动化水平显著提高。水利信息广域网不断扩展，骨干网络与地市水利部门联通率达到63.1%，部分省（自治区、直辖市）实现了区县级水利部门的全覆盖。国家防汛抗旱指挥系统一期工程建设进入收尾阶段，全国水土保持监测网络和信息系统一期工程完成，全国24个城市开展了水资源实时监控与管理系统建设试点，29个大型灌区开展了信息化试点。全国防汛卫星通信网基本建成，遥感技术已广泛应用于灾害性天气预报和水旱灾害监测，以地理信息系统技术为支撑的水利空间数据建设、管理和业务应用迅速展开，全球定位系统在大江大河的水下地形测量中得到实际应用，视频会议系统在防汛抗旱远程会商和指挥调度过程中发挥了突出作用，可视化技术正逐步应用于流域和水利对象的跟踪、模拟展示与管理，越来越多的数学模型、分析软件在水利工作中得到应用。当前和今后一个时期，加快水利信息化步伐，以水利信息化带动水利现代化，是一项事关水利发展全局的重大战略任务。

The information system for water sector commenced at the mid and late 1970s. In recent years, due to adhering to the principle of pushing water modernization with informationization, a comprehensive information system composed of basic infrastructure, applied system and supportive environment has been formed. And computer communication and network technologies have been widely applied achieving automatic and 24-hour acquisition, transmission, storage and processing of data. The hydrological data base is being developed rapidly and capacity to serve the public increased dramatically, which have provoked the transition from the traditional to the modern and sustainable water management.

More than 27,000 data acquisition stations have been constructed among which automatic stations account for 47.5% and accuracy, timeliness, effectiveness and automation of system supervision and control have been significantly improved. The water information network keeps extending and the connections between backbone net

and local water agencies has reached 63.1% and in some provinces and municipalities the network has connected all county level water administrative agencies. The Phase I of the State Flood Control and Drought Relief Commanding System has almost come to the ending period, and the National Water and Soil Conservation Monitoring Network and Information System (Phase I) has been completed. 24 cities have undertaken pilots for water resources real-time supervision and management system while 29 large-scale irrigation districts have started pilot projects for information system. The flood control satellite communication system has been basically set up, and remote sensing technology widely used for forecasting catastrophic weather and monitoring floods and droughts. The development, management and application of water spatial data with GIS have been developed. The GPS has been used for underwater geographic survey and investigation of large rivers. Visual consultation meeting system has played a striking role in consultation and commanding, regulation of flood prevention and drought relief. Visualized technology is gradually being applied in tracking, simulating, displaying and management of river basins and water objectives. More and more mathematic models and analytical software are introduced and used in daily routine work. At present and time to come, it is a crucial strategic task concerned to overall development of water sector to speed up water information development and pushing water modernization with water informationization.

① 国家防汛抗旱总指挥部异地视频会议系统
The Remote Consultation Meeting System in the State Flood Control and Drought Relief Headquarters' office

② 大黑汀水库大坝视频监控信息采集设备
The Visual Monitoring and Dam Data Collection System in Daheiting Reservoir

③ 水利信息网网络示意图
The Figure of Water Information Network

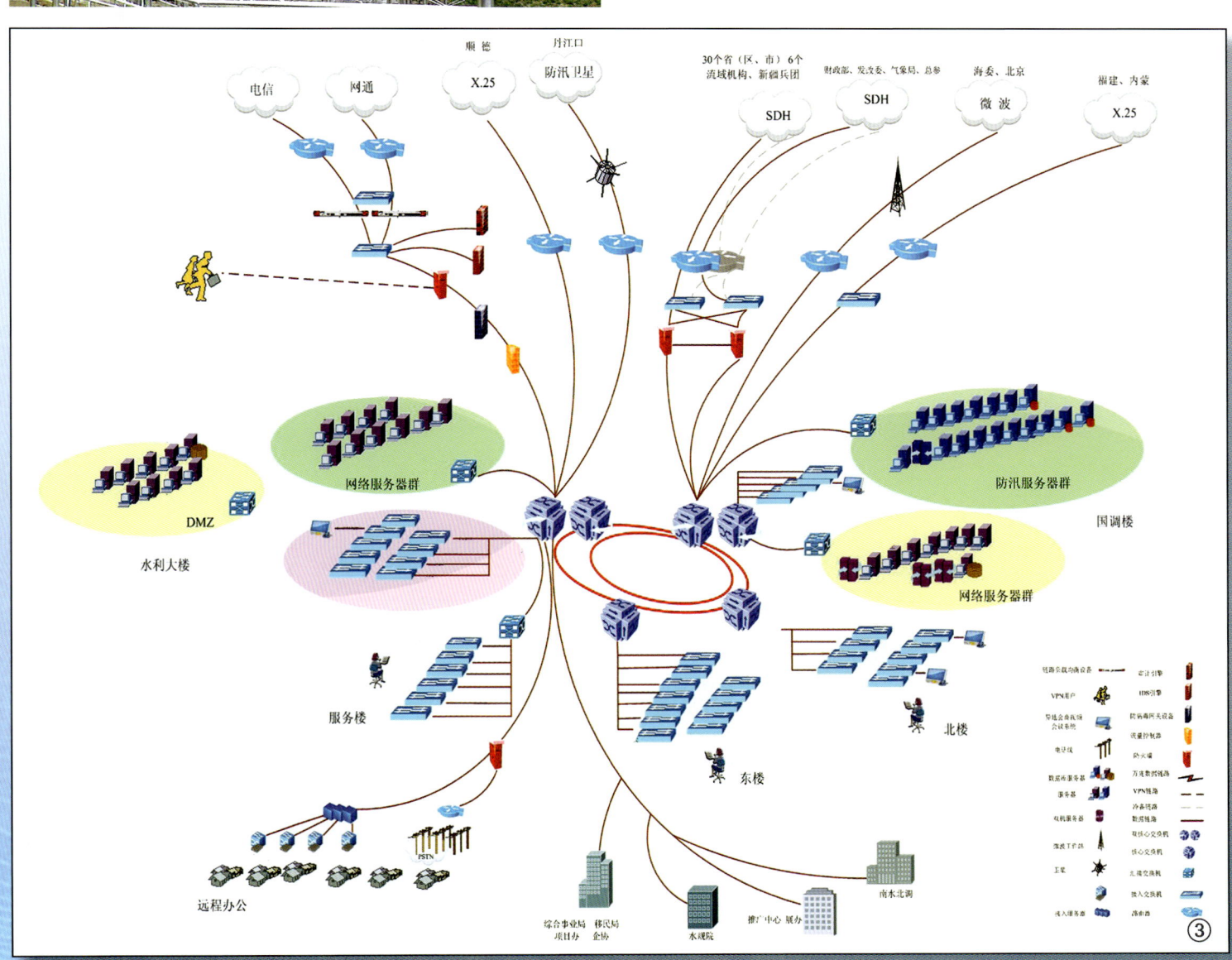

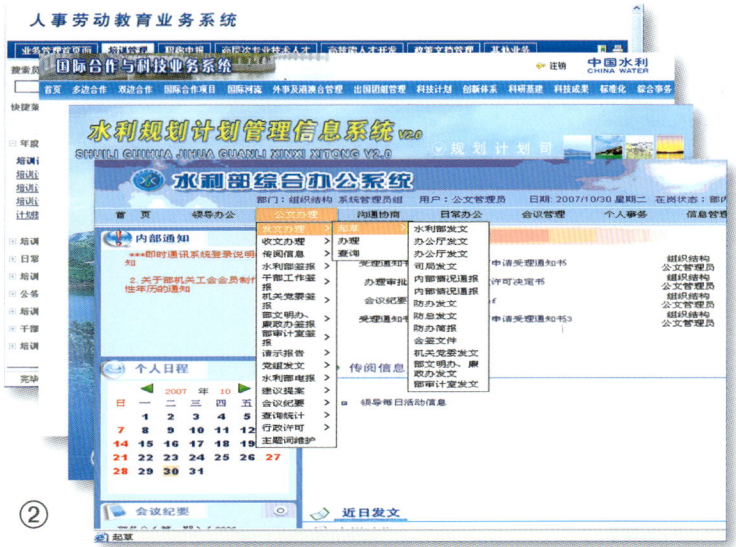
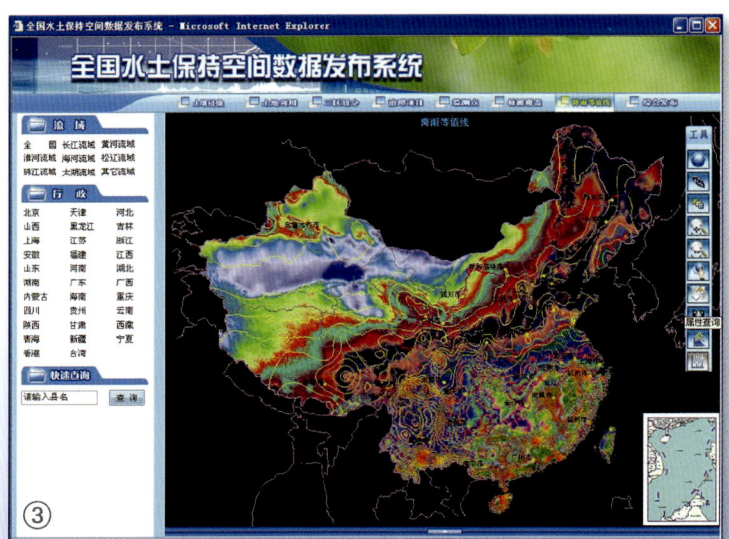

① 全国防汛水雨情信息系统
The National Flood Control & Water Regime Information System

② 水利电子政务系统
The E-government system of water sector

③ 全国水土保持空间数据发布系统
The Spatial Data System for National Water and Soil Conservation

④ 全国1:25万水利基础电子地图发布系统
National Electrical Image System for Water Sector at scale of 1:250,000

⑤ 水利部水利信息中心对全国水利信息网运行情况进行监测
The Information Center of the MWR for monitoring the operation of the National Water Information Net

⑥ 黄河水量调度中心
The Water Volume Regulation Center of the Yellow River Basin

⑦ MODIS数据发布与水利应用系统
Platform for MODIS Data Displaying and Application

⑧ 太湖流域蓝藻遥感监测图
Remote Sensing Image of Green Algae in the Taihu Lake Basin

Chapter V  Science, Technology and Innovation    第五篇  科技与创新

⑥

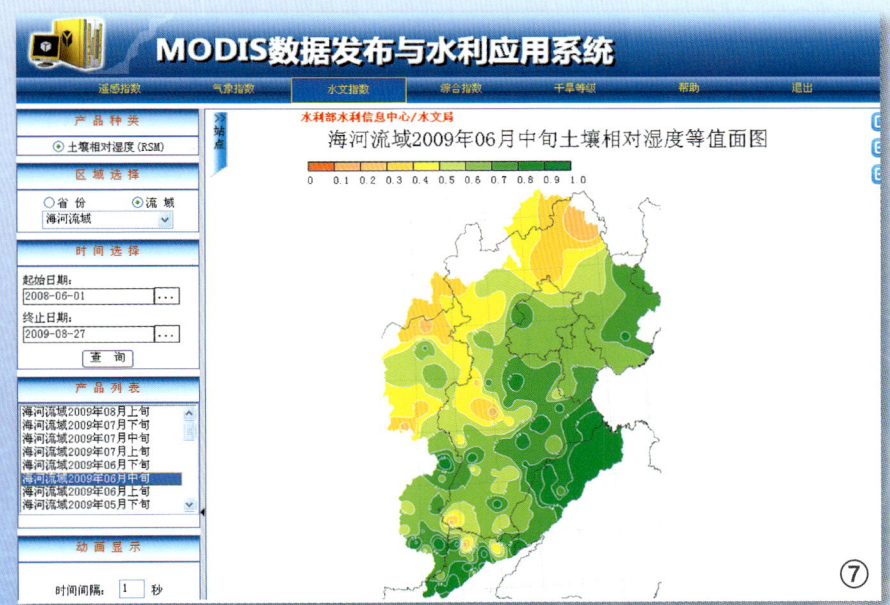
⑦

⑧

0101
1010
0101
1001
1001
0101
1011
0111

# 后记

60年风雨兼程，60年春华秋实。经过新中国成立以来的大规模建设特别是经过改革开放30年的跨越式发展，我国防洪减灾、供水保障和水土资源保护等方面的能力明显提高，有力地保障了防洪安全、供水安全、粮食安全和生态安全，促进了经济社会的可持续发展。

当前和今后一个时期，是全面建设小康社会、加快推进社会主义现代化建设的重要时期，也是推进传统水利向现代水利、可持续发展水利转变的关键时期。人多水少、水资源时空分布不均、水土资源和生产力布局不相匹配，依然是现阶段我国的突出水情；资源环境对经济增长的约束，依然是我国发展过程中面临的突出矛盾；干旱缺水、洪涝灾害、水污染和水土流失等问题，依然是制约我国经济社会可持续发展的突出因素；水资源管理体制不顺和水利发展机制不活，依然是水利发展道路上的突出障碍。

我们要深刻认识和准确把握水利发展的这些阶段性特征，进一步深入贯彻落实科学发展观，积极践行可持续发展治水思路，围绕实现全面建设小康社会奋斗目标的新要求，大力倡导以人为本、人与自然和谐的治水理念，加快推进水利基础设施建设，着力解决涉及民生的水利问题，全面落实最严格的水资源管理制度，继续深化水利各项改革，进一步提升水利保障能力。到2020年基本建成重点流域和区域综合防洪减灾体系、城乡水资源合理配置和高效利用体系、水环境保护和河湖生态健康保障体系、较为完善的管理和运行保障体系，人民群众的防洪安全将得到可靠保障，城乡居民普遍享有安全清洁的饮用水，水环境和水生态状况显著改善，中国的山更绿、水更清、天更蓝，一个充满生机和活力的现代水利蓝图将在我们的手中变成现实。

# Epilogue

With 60 years of devotion and hardworking since 1949, particularly after the leap-frog development in the last 30 years, the capacity of flood control and disaster mitigation, water supply, water and land resources protection, etc. has been improved significantly, thus providing robust support to achieve safety of flood control, water supply, food production and ecology and promoting the sustainable development of the economy and the society.

For now and in the near future, it is a crucial period to build a moderately prosperous society in all respects, speed up the building-up of socialist modernization and further promote the transition from traditional water resources management to the modernized and sustainable one. The large population with finite water resources, uneven distribution of water resources in both time and space, un-matching between the availability of water and land resources and productivity layout remain as the outstanding features. The constrain on economic development by resources and environment is still the prevailing contradiction. The droughts and water scarcity, floods and waterlogging, water pollution and, water and soil erosion keep as constraining factors to the sustainable development of society and economy. On the way forward of development for water sector, water resources institutions and water development mechanisms need to be further improved.

We have to fully recognize and accurately master these periodical characteristics of water development, implement in-depth scientific development concept, put the sustainable water development into practice in broader areas. We shall advocate and promote the human-oriented water management philosophy and the harmony between human and nature in line with new requirements of construction of the well-off society in all-round ways, focus on addressing water issues related to people's livelihood, implement the strictest water resources management system in an overall manner, continue reforms in water sector to improve water supportive and guaranteeing capacity. By 2020, the comprehensive flood control and disaster mitigation system for major river basins and regions, rural and urban water resources rational distribution and high-efficiency systems, water environment protection and river-lake ecological healthy systems, the improved managerial and operational systems shall be basically completed. By that time, flood control safety shall be ensured, and residents in both rural and urban areas shall enjoy safe, and clean drinking water. Water environment and ecological status shall be improved significantly. The greener mountains, cleaner water, bluer sky and a modern water blueprint full of vigor and vitality will come into being.

# 新中国中央水行政主管部门及主要领导人
## Water Administrating Institutions at Central Level and Successive Leaders of the People's Republic of China

| 机构<br>Institution | 主要领导人<br>Principal Leader | 任职时间<br>Time of Appointment |
|---|---|---|
| 中华人民共和国水利部<br>Ministry of Water Conservancy of the People's Republic of China | 傅作义<br>Fu Zuoyi | 1949年10月<br>October 1949 |
| 中华人民共和国水利电力部<br>Ministry of Water Conservancy and Electric Power of the People's Republic of China | 傅作义<br>Fu Zuoyi | 1958年2月<br>February 1958 |
| 中华人民共和国水利电力部<br>（军管会）<br>Ministry of Water Conservancy and Electric Power of the People's Republic of China<br>(Military Control Committee) | 陈德三<br>（主任）<br>Chen Desan<br>(Director) | 1967年7月<br>July 1967 |
| 中华人民共和国水利电力部<br>（革委会、军管会）<br>Ministry of Water Conservancy and Electric Power of the People's Republic of China<br>(Revolutionary Committee, Military Control Committee) | 张文碧<br>（主任）<br>Zhang Wenbi<br>(Director) | 1970年1月<br>January 1970 |
| 中华人民共和国水利电力部<br>Ministry of Water Conservancy and Electric Power of the People's Republic of China | 钱正英<br>Qian Zhengying | 1975年1月<br>January 1975 |
| 中华人民共和国水利部<br>Ministry of Water Resources of the People's Republic of China | 钱正英<br>Qian Zhengying | 1979年2月<br>February 1979 |
| 中华人民共和国水利电力部<br>Ministry of Water Resources and Electric Power of the People's Republic of China | 钱正英<br>Qian Zhengying | 1982年3月<br>March 1982 |
| 中华人民共和国水利部<br>Ministry of Water Resources of the People's Republic of China | 杨振怀<br>Yang Zhenhuai | 1988年5月<br>May 1988 |
| | 钮茂生<br>Niu Maosheng | 1993年3月<br>March 1993 |
| | 汪恕诚<br>Wang Shucheng | 1998年11月<br>November 1998 |
| | 陈 雷<br>Chen Lei | 2007年4月<br>April 2007 |

## 新中国历任和现任水利部长
### Ministers of Water Resources, P. R. China

傅作义
Fu Zuoyi

钱正英
Qian Zhengying

杨振怀
Yang Zhenhuai

钮茂生
Niu Maosheng

汪恕诚
Wang Shucheng

陈　雷
Chen Lei

# 编纂委员会

## 主 任
陈 雷

## 副主任
鄂竟平　董 力
矫 勇　周 英　胡四一
刘 宁　陈小江

## 委 员
汪 洪　周学文　赵 伟　孙雪涛
张红兵　刘雅鸣　高 波　孙继昌
刘 震　王晓东　王爱国　刘学钊
王 星　何源满　张志彤　田中兴

## 主 编
陈小江

## 副主编
汤鑫华　吴文庆　陈东明

## 参编人员
李训喜　李中锋　张 范　曲大鹏
夏明勇　纪 红　江文涛　王 凯
刘宝勤　李丽艳　韩莹琳　侯林英
殷海军　刘媛媛　刘 巍　邹 昱

## 英文翻译
郝 钏　徐 静　王晋苏　邬全丰

## 英文校译
孟志敏　郑如刚

## 图片拍摄

（按姓氏笔画排序）

丁福俊　王凤奎　王建民　王梦祥　王连生
白　江　白金宝　龙　虎　刘一燊　刘大伟
刘凤岐　刘柏良　孙仁贵　朱卫东　朱春雷
池晓虹　何希斌　张　宪　张　锐　张进平
张建华　李　刚　李小可　李先明　杨子江
杨争红　汪　栋　辛仁健　邹幼勤　孟令钦
孟宪玉　林　耕　罗胜利　姜拥军　胡顺华
贺道富　晋知华　殷鹤仙　秦　刚　高　群
焉学义　黄　皓　黄正平　黄国贵　黄宝林
黄爱民　董保华　蒋长树　韩学章　熊志刚
缪宜江　谭少明　潘　征　潘刚卡　等

### 责任编辑

马爱梅　张　洁

### 装帧设计

王　鹏　李　菲　芦　博　刘一燊　何玉晓
丁一殊　冯　强　钱　诚　李晔韬

### 地图校核

樊启玲　黄云燕

### 责任校对

张　莉　黄淑娜　梁晓静　黄　梅

### 责任印制

黄勇忠　焦　岩

### 图书在版编目（CIP）数据

兴利除害　富国惠民：新中国水利60年 = Generate Benefits and Mitigate Hazards to Contribute to the Prosperity of the Nation and the Interests of the People:60 Years' Water Development in China / 中华人民共和国水利部编. -- 北京：中国水利水电出版社，2009.9
ISBN 978-7-5084-6500-5

Ⅰ. ①兴… Ⅱ. ①中… Ⅲ. ①水利建设－成就－中国－1949～2009－画册 Ⅳ. ①F426.9-64

中国版本图书馆CIP数据核字（2009）第168543号

本书中的地图由中国地图出版社提供，地图上中国国界线系按照中国地图出版社1989年出版的1:400万《中华人民共和国地形图》绘制。

审图号：GS（2009）1393号

| | |
|---|---|
| 书　名 | **兴利除害　富国惠民——新中国水利60年**<br>Generate Benefits and Mitigate Hazards to Contribute to the Prosperity of the Nation and the Interests of the People — 60 Years' Water Development in China |
| 作　者 | 中华人民共和国水利部　编<br>Compiled by the Ministry of Water Resources, P. R. China |
| 出版发行 | 中国水利水电出版社　（北京市海淀区玉渊潭南路1号D座　100038）<br>网　　址：www.waterpub.com.cn<br>E-mail：sales@waterpub.com.cn<br>电　　话：(010) 68367658 (营销中心) |
| 经　售 | 北京科水图书销售中心（零售）<br>电　　话：(010) 88383994、63202643<br>全国各地新华书店和相关出版物销售网点 |
| 排　版 | 中国水利水电出版社装帧出版部 |
| 印　刷 | 北京雅昌彩色印刷有限公司 |
| 规　格 | 255 mm×355 mm　8开本　31.5印张　380千字 |
| 版　次 | 2009年9月第1版　2009年9月第1次印刷 |
| 印　数 | 0001—3000 册 |
| 定　价 | 580.00元（附光盘1张） |

凡购买我社图书，如有缺页、倒页、脱页的，本社营销中心负责调换

**版权所有·侵权必究**